ON DARK AND BLOODY GROUND

ANNE T. LAWRENCE

ON DARK AND BLOODY GROUND

AN ORAL HISTORY OF THE WEST VIRGINIA MINE WARS

With a Foreword by
CATHERINE VENABLE MOORE

West Virginia University Press / Morgantown

First edition published 2021 by West Virginia University Press
Printed in the United States of America

ISBN 978-1-952271-08-3 (cloth) / 978-1-952271-09-0 (paperback) /
978-1-952271-10-6 (ebook)

Library of Congress Control Number: 2021009486

Book and cover design by Than Saffel
Cover art from *End Grain*, by Aaron Hughes. Used with permission.

All royalties from the sale of this book go to support the West Virginia Mine
Wars Museum.

www.wvminewars.com

CONTENTS

FOREWORD

When I discovered *On Dark and Bloody Ground (ODABG)* in the library—one of only two copies located in the state of West Virginia at the time—I knew immediately that I'd struck a rich vein of voice and story.

For months I'd been immersed in U.S. Senate testimony and court transcripts of the treason trials that arose from the Battle of Blair Mountain in 1921, when as many as ten thousand armed unionist coal miners marched into a remote area of nonunion territory and went to war with the coal establishment of southern West Virginia: coal operators and the deputy sheriffs on their payroll, armed private mine guards, and community members from Logan County and the surrounding areas who opposed the union.

Those formal testimonies were undoubtedly precious recordings, but they were delivered under the intense scrutiny of corporate lawyers, U.S. Senators, and other white men in suits. *On Dark and Bloody Ground* was something different—people, often in their own homes, and always on their own terms, telling stories of what they did and saw and understood about the battle and the many skirmishes that led up to it. They included some of the primary participants in the conflict, and importantly, a number of women.

It was like reading a *Spoon River Anthology* or an *Our Town* about the Battle of Blair Mountain and the mine wars: a composite photo made up of many smaller portraits, a landscape textured with actual life. You could see the events from a number of different angles. You could see how real life isn't always clear cut or black and white; that it isn't always a strict Us vs. Them—there are gradations, and human fallibility, and people whose memories and perspectives evolve and change over time.

When I found the manuscript, I was working with the board of the West Virginia Mine Wars Museum in Matewan, West Virginia; the United Mine Workers of America; and other community leaders across the region to organize a statewide commemoration of the Battle of Blair Mountain Centennial, scheduled for Labor Day weekend of 2021. Our museum is one of the key current day repositories for the collective memory of the mine wars, and one of our founding goals was to provide educators with resources to teach this history in their classrooms. I imagined how exciting it would be to reprint the book somehow, since the text might be useful as a teaching tool—or a souvenir for the big centennial—but a Google search for the author's name, Anne Lawrence, produced seemingly endless results, so tracking her down felt hopeless. Yet, a few days later, out of the clear blue, Anne emailed the museum asking if we wanted an old copy of the publication that she had found among her papers. We were overjoyed to hear from her, and the republication project was soon under way. Anne gave us permission to reproduce her material, and she asked that any royalties earned be donated to the West Virginia Mine Wars Museum. We are grateful for her generosity.

By the time the interviews in *ODABG* were recorded, it had been fifty years since the Battle of Blair Mountain; the United Mine Workers of America (UMWA) had been embraced in southern West Virginia and succeeded in many of its goals, like promoting education, offering access to health care, and generally contributing to a rising standard of living among mining families. And crucially, people were now willing to talk about the mine wars publicly. Previously there had been taboos, shame, and fears of imprisonment to contend with, so participating families hadn't discussed the events much, even among themselves. It wasn't uncommon for those who'd been involved to split town altogether, as several of these narratives attest. Perhaps the project itself helped in some small way to break the taboo.

As Anne and I worked to compile this book, she told me more about the origins of the oral history project and how she gathered the interviews. In early 1972, the *Miner's Voice*, a labor newspaper published by the Appalachian Public Interest Journalism Group under the editorship of Don Stillman, received a grant from the National Endowment for the Humanities to encourage young people's interest in the humanities. They proposed conducting an oral history with the men and women who'd participated in the unionization of the coalfields of Central Appalachia during the 1920s and 1930s.

The Miner's Voice—a mouthpiece for the Miners for Democracy movement, which sought to root out corruption in the UMWA—hired Anne, a junior at Swarthmore College studying sociology and history, to direct the project. She moved to Charleston, West Virginia, and from June to October 1972, she traveled through the coalfields of central and southern West Virginia, eastern Kentucky, and southwestern Virginia, seeking out and interviewing mostly retired miners and their wives about their union experiences. She focused on a few key historical events and periods, including the Battle of Blair Mountain. The eyewitnesses were mostly elderly folks who had been teenagers or young adults at the time. Others reported stories they had heard from older members of the community, or from family. She made many of her initial contacts through individuals active in the community of retired miners, including leaders of the Black Lung Association and people who collected burial fund dues. She also drew on networks of union reformers, VISTA volunteers, journalists, and academic researchers. Individuals she interviewed introduced her to an ever-expanding web of old timers who witnessed this history firsthand and were willing to go public with their stories.

In most cases, Anne spent hours—and sometimes days—developing rapport before conducting the taped interview. Most interviews took place at the subject's home, but some occurred at senior centers and other places where older people socialized in the community. Eventually, Anne gathered about one hundred hours of tape-recorded interviews with more than eighty retired miners and their family members.

After some experimentation, she prepared one entry per person for the final report, a typescript volume dated January 1973. Instead of simply compiling the unedited transcripts, she placed direct quotations from the tape recordings alongside cinematic descriptions of physical setting, interviewees' appearance and personality, and historical information. She grouped the entries by region, prefacing each with brief sections of historical context, and titled it *On Dark and Bloody Ground: An Oral History of the U.M.W.A. in Central Appalachia 1920–1935*—so named for a ghostly and apocryphal description of Kentucky from oral tradition, most likely referencing the blood of Iroquois warriors slaughtered during battle with white settler-colonials. This abridged edition includes only those interviews relevant to the mine wars in West Virginia.

When I first read the material reproduced here, I was particularly moved by the picture that it painted of the eventual organization of Logan County by the UMWA, deep in the heart of the Great Depression. Of what a relief it was; of the stealthy way in which the organizing campaign was carried out; of how immediately its value was evident in people's lives.

"The difference working in a nonunion mine and a union mine was like jumping out of the fire into a cool stream of water," recalled Kelly Buchanan, one of the people Anne interviewed. "Before it was every dog eat dog. When you go into anything collectively, everybody is striving to do the same thing. That's the only way you can have peace in the coalfields."

"The miner, he had always been kind of like a slave in everyone's opinion, even his own," said Edward Perry. The union was a chance "to come up, not to accept it laying down, but to come up to a place in society where they was acceptable, by their striving—"

Once again, that word, "striving."

"—And they've got it, too. It was by the older miners having these sentiments of equality, that's why working miners today are accepted in any society."

"Honey, I really know what the union is," one of the interviewees said simply. "All of us old fellows do, the ones that fought for it."

Looking around at my home in West Virginia in 2017, sometimes I wondered if we knew anymore.

And then the following year, the state's teachers and school employees banded their three unions together and went on strike, reminding us all what union looks like, and what it can accomplish. When I arrived on the steps of the State Capitol on that cold, wet February day to witness their strike announcement, I saw a tent emblazoned with the seal of the United Mine Workers of America standing in solidarity at center stage; I met strikers whose grandparents had fought on the rugged ridges of Blair Mountain; I heard fiery speeches quoting Mary "Mother" Jones, the "Miner's Angel," who a century earlier had inspired West Virginia's colliers to band together and break the chains of their social and economic oppression. "Solidarity is the foundation of our country, the foundation of our unions and the foundation of our freedom," boomed Levi Allen, the UMWA's young secretary-treasurer. "The most powerful word in the Constitution of the United States of America is only two letters and it's the first word: We, we, we! When we come together, we can do extraordinary things." And he was right. In the end, the school employees' technically illegal thirteen-day strike resulted in a 5 percent pay raise for *all* public workers in West Virginia—they deserved even more, but they'd achieved something beyond a modest raise. They'd reminded those in the statehouse that legislators are indeed servants of the people, and they'd reasserted their own power, dignity, and self-respect in the face of dehumanizing working conditions.

Significantly, those fighting on the front lines of labor in 2018 were largely women, and they didn't dig coal or assemble widgets or write code; they worked in the public service sector, the top employer in nearly all of our rural counties. These were women who worked low-paying jobs as cooks, teachers, and social workers on the front lines of the addiction crisis and who addressed the ongoing economic hardship of many of our most vulnerable residents. And their strike was about pay and affordable health insurance, yes, but it was also about the right to a quality public education for young West Virginians. Among the strikers I spoke to, it always came down to that: educating, bettering, striving.

Many wore red bandannas as a symbol of solidarity, and a nod to the men and women who a hundred years ago stood up for similar beliefs and values.

We hope this new edition does justice to both the miners and these school employees, and that it will serve as a reminder to us all that when its power is wielded strategically, "the union makes us strong."

Catherine Venable Moore
West Virginia Mine Wars Museum
Matewan, WV

ACKNOWLEDGMENTS

I conducted the interviews and prepared the manuscript titled *On Dark and Bloody Ground: An Oral History of the U.M.W.A. in Central Appalachia 1920–1935* in 1972, when I was a twenty-one-year-old student on leave from Swarthmore College. I am grateful to many people who helped me at that time, and to others who helped me more recently—almost fifty years later—to bring this volume to publication.

The original interviews were conducted with the financial support of a Youthgrant from the National Endowment for the Humanities. Its purpose was to collect oral histories of the unionization of the Appalachian coalfields in the 1920s and 1930s. The grant recipient was the *Miner's Voice*, a newspaper published by the Appalachian Public Interest Research Group in support of the Miners for Democracy, the reform movement in the United Mine Workers of America. I am grateful to Amy Totenberg, then on the staff of the *Miner's Voice*, for recommending me, and to the newspaper's editor, Don Stillman, who hired me to direct the oral history project.

Librarians at West Virginia University, the West Virginia Archives of History, the Historical Reading Room of the Kanawha Public Library, and the Library of Congress assisted with my background research. Professors William Weinberg of Alice Lloyd College and Helen Clinch of Clinch Valley State College helped school me in the techniques of oral history. Edgar James, my first teacher of West Virginia history, loaned me his book collection.

Many people assisted me as I traveled around the coalfields with my portable tape recorder and miniature cassettes, searching for people who had witnessed the mineworkers union's origins. I am grateful to dozens of union reformers, VISTA volunteers, academic researchers, black lung activists, bluegrass musicians, and community organizers who pointed the way to "old timers" in their midst, who in turn pointed the way to others.

Matt Witt arranged for the publication of excerpts from four of these interviews in a special history edition of the *United Mine Workers Journal* in January 1974, when he was then the associate editor. The four photographs published here accompanied that issue.

More recently, James Humphreys introduced me to the staff of the Gelman Library at George Washington University, which is now the repository of my original tape recordings. Vakil Smallen, the library's labor history archivist, has overseen their digitization and transcription.

Earl Dotter has been my guide to historical photographs of the period and restored the four photographs of interviewees reproduced here from the *United Mine Workers Journal*.

Emily Marsh of Colorbox Industries prepared the original maps included in this volume.

This book would not have been possible without the support of Catherine Venable Moore, who discovered my original *On Dark and Bloody Ground* manuscript and who encouraged me to republish it in connection with the hundred-year anniversary of the Battle of Blair Mountain. She brought to this project her deep knowledge of West Virginia history and boundless creative energy.

Above all, I am grateful to the women and men who opened their homes and hearts to me to share their stories of the West Virginia mine wars.

INTRODUCTION

The interviews included in *On Dark and Bloody Ground* focus on a tumultuous period in West Virginia labor history, roughly spanning the years 1912 to 1933. During these two decades, coal miners fought—sometimes violently—in defense of their rights and for union recognition in the face of intense opposition from coal operators and their allies. The geographic scope of the interviews ranges from Kanawha County southward and westward into Boone, Raleigh, Logan, and Mingo Counties.

These eyewitness accounts, recorded in 1972, spotlight two pivotal events. In 1921, union miners from the Kanawha coalfield in central West Virginia organized an armed march to support their brothers and sisters to their south who were fighting for union recognition. The march, which culminated in the week-long Battle of Blair Mountain, ended when President Warren G. Harding dispatched U.S. Army troops to break up the conflict, prompting both sides to peacefully surrender. In 1933, following the passage of the National Industrial Recovery Act, which granted workers the right to organize, the United Mine Workers of America (UMWA) sent organizers into the southern coalfields of West Virginia, where thousands of miners flocked to "take the obligation"—the oath of union membership.

The interviews collectively tell the story of the rise of organized labor in southern West Virginia. They start with a union defeat in the aftermath of the Battle of Blair Mountain. They end with a union victory as organizers swept through Logan and adjacent counties and won their first contracts.

The history of this era has been ably documented by several labor historians and journalists, including James Green, Lon Savage, Robert Shogan, David A. Corbin, and Rebecca J. Bailey. A full list of resources is provided at the end of this book. This introduction will provide a brief synopsis of events and three conceptual maps created for this book to help the reader situate the stories told here in the broader context of historical events.

The history of the coal miners' union in West Virginia is layered upon the geology of coal formations in the Appalachian mountain range. The state is home to several major coal deposits, including the Kanawha, Logan (also called the Guyan), and Williamson fields, as shown in map 1. Each field had many mines, communities of people who made their living from the industry, and railroads that carried coal to distant markets. Map 2 shows the location of county lines, major waterways, and, for reference, some of the key communities mentioned in the interviews.

The UMWA first succeeded in organizing the coalfields in the northern and central parts of the state, as workers from unionized mines in Pennsylvania and elsewhere brought with them their experiences with organized labor. One of the first UMWA organizers was Mary "Mother" Jones, who helped lead strikes in the Kanawha and New River coalfields in 1902 and again in 1912–13. (The New River coalfield is farther to the east and not shown in map 1.) The struggles to build the union in these regions created a legacy of strong union families, from which many labor and community leaders later emerged.

As the UMWA sought to spread its influence south into Mingo County, miners there struck in 1920 for union recognition. Operators responded by hiring armed private detectives from the Baldwin-Felts agency, bringing in scabs to work the mines, and

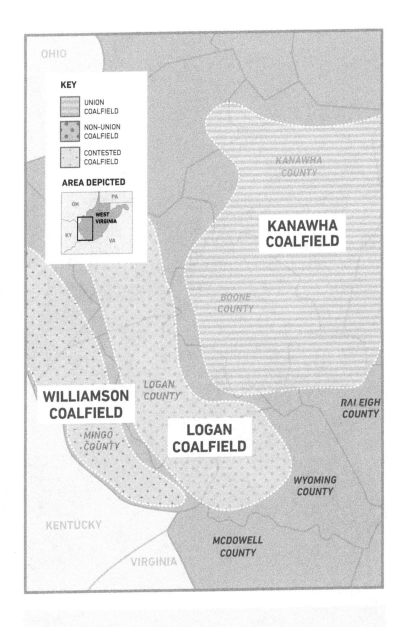

Map 1. Southern West Virginia Coalfields, Patterns of Unionization, 1921
(Map by Colorbox Industries)

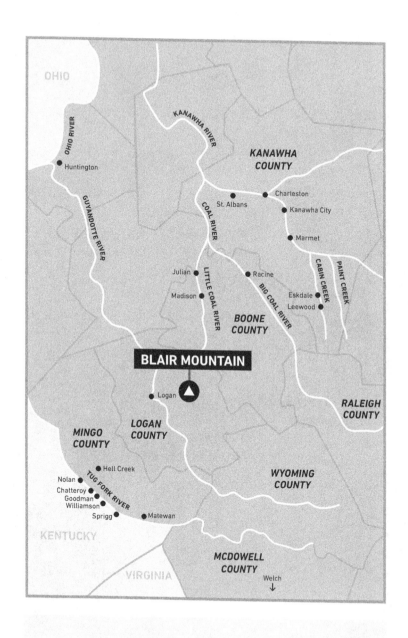

Map 2. Southern West Virginia, Rivers, Counties, and Selected Communities
(Map by Colorbox Industries)

evicting miners and their families from company housing—forcing them into tent colonies along the Tug Fork River. In some instances, miners were jailed for failure to follow martial law.

In May 1920, the chief of police in Matewan, Sid Hatfield, a union supporter, accompanied by the town's mayor and a group of angry miners, attempted to stop the ongoing evictions. Near the railroad depot, they confronted a group of Baldwin-Felts agents, and gunfire erupted. When the shoot-out was over, ten people, including the mayor, seven Baldwin-Felts agents, and two miners had been fatally wounded.

Just over a year later, Hatfield and his deputy Ed Chambers were lured into a trap and murdered by another group of Baldwin-Felts agents on the steps of the courthouse in Welch, in nearby McDowell County, incensing union supporters across the region. The strike dragged on, with both sides locked in.

In adjacent Logan County, the union had made little headway. There, coal operators paid Sheriff Don Chafin a royalty based on tonnage to support himself and more than forty armed deputies to keep out the union by any means necessary. Chafin's deputies terrorized the coal camps and patrolled the railroad stations, throwing out any arrivals suspected of union sympathies. By 1921, Chafin had accumulated a personal net worth of about $5 million in today's dollars from his work for the operators.

On April 1, 1921, the temporary contract covering the unionized mines in the Kanawha coalfield expired, and miners struck for a new contract. Afraid of price competition from coal produced by cheap labor, the Kanawha operators responded by stipulating that they would not renew the contract unless the mines to the south were also forced to pay union-scale wages.

Miners met in mass gatherings all through the central part of the state to develop a unified strategy. Led by a core of strong unionists from the Cabin Creek area, the miners decided to stage a military invasion of Logan and Mingo Counties. They had mixed motivations—to avenge the deaths of Hatfield and Chambers, to free union miners who had been jailed in Mingo County, and to protect their own working conditions by forcing the southern operators to recognize the union.

The miners' march, as it was called, was planned with military precision. Supporters organized squads to supply food and medical care to the marching miners. They commandeered a C&O passenger train at gunpoint to transport the men. They sent messengers to places as far away as Illinois and Ohio to recruit armed supporters. Ammunition was purchased with the assistance of a sympathetic Charleston merchant, possibly with cash provided by unionized coal operators. As many as 10,000 men may have joined the march.

Sheriff Chafin hastily assembled a force of hundreds of deputies, middle-class residents, and some miners who were pressed into duty, and sent them up to the mountain ridge near the town of Blair on the eastern border of Logan County. There, they dug trenches and prepared to withstand what they viewed as an attack by an army of lawless criminals. Chafin's forces, too, were heavily armed—in part by the Kentucky governor, who had sent trainloads of machine guns and high-powered rifles.

The two groups met on Blair Mountain, a ridge that divided the watersheds of the Guyandotte and Coal Rivers—and, not incidentally, the union and nonunion coalfields. There, they battled for five days, exchanging fire from their entrenched positions and engaging in occasional hand-to-hand skirmishes, probably killing or wounding dozens of men on both sides. By the end of the week, the union forces were on the verge of breaking through Chafin's defensive lines and down the other side of the mountain.

By this time, state officials had become increasingly alarmed. At the urgent request of the West Virginia governor, President Warren G. Harding dispatched U.S. Army troops to Huntington, where they divided into two units. One came down the Coal River to cut off the miners' forces, the other journeyed down the Guyandotte River to cut off the defenders. The army brought in a train to carry the miners home. The marchers complied. Notably, many were World War I veterans. Despite their union militance, they were fiercely patriotic men, and they were unwilling to fight U.S. soldiers.

Map 3 depicts the Battle of Blair Mountain, showing the routes of the union and anti-union forces, the location of major skirmishes, and the movements of the U.S. Army troops. It also shows various communities and creeks mentioned in the interviews.

As a result of their compliance, the miners in the Kanawha field lost their union contract, and the miners in Mingo County lost their strike. The repercussions of these defeats ricocheted across the region. Without Logan and its adjacent counties in its column, the UMWA could not win any concessions from the fiercely competitive operators, and the union simply collapsed. In West Virginia, the membership of the UMWA dropped from 50,000 members in 1920 to 600 in 1929.

The Great Depression hit the coal communities of southern West Virginia with a vengeance. Many mines closed, and the distressed owners of the ones hanging on slashed wages and hours. By 1933, more than a third of all miners were earning less than $2.50 a day. Many worked only one or two days a week. Men roamed the region looking for odd jobs, and families cultivated vegetable patches along the hillsides above the company towns. Their crops of corn, potatoes, beans, and tomatoes often made the difference between subsistence and starvation.

The system of professional thugs was still a menace and still flourishing in the coal camps, but under these conditions miners' fear of the companies and their retainers began to recede. The few men who had formerly worked in union mines began, for the first time in a decade, to talk among their friends and neighbors. Men would travel in secrecy from house to house, spreading the word about the union. Small groups began meeting regularly in the woods, or in private homes where company guards could not enter.

In 1933, national legislation finally shifted the balance of power in the coalfields. That year President Franklin D. Roosevelt, with the active encouragement of UMWA president John L.

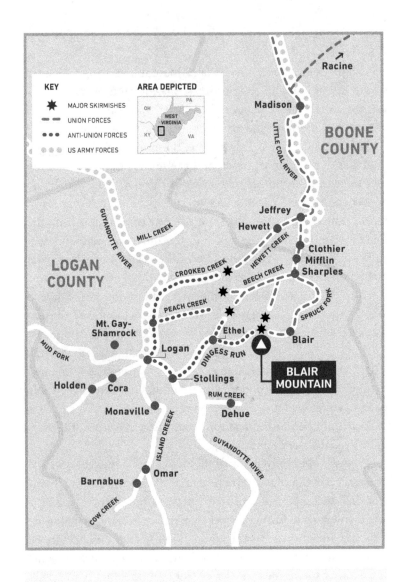

Racine

Madison

BOONE
COUNTY

LITTLE COAL RIVER

Jeffrey

Hewett

Clothier
Mifflin
Sharples

HEWETT CREEK
BEECH CREEK

MILL CREEK

GUYANDOTTE RIVER

LOGAN
COUNTY

CROOKED CREEK

SPRUCE FORK

PEACH CREEK

Mt. Gay-
Shamrock

Ethel

Blair

MUD FORK

Logan

DINGESS RUN

BLAIR
MOUNTAIN

Holden   Cora

Stollings

RUM CREEK

Monaville

Dehue

ISLAND CREEK

GUYANDOTTE RIVER

Barnabus   Omar

COW CREEK

Map 3. The Battle of Blair Mountain and Surrounding Communities, 1921
(Map by Colorbox Industries)

Lewis, supported—and Congress passed—the National Industrial Recovery Act, which recognized labor's right to organize.

Lewis seized on this opportunity to rebuild his disintegrated organization. Legally protected for the first time, union organizers swept through Logan County in 1933. A massive meeting was called at the Ellis ballpark. The men had been waiting for years, and they turned out by the thousands. The miners repeated the oath in unison after their chanting leaders. Even Tennis Hatfield—Don Chafin's successor—turned up. But this time, the miners had the upper hand, and they ran him out of the ballpark.

The southern West Virginia operators, faced with the coalition of miners, the UMWA, and the U.S. government, capitulated and recognized the union. The miners had finally jumped out of the fire—and into the cool stream of union power. This book tells this story in the words of some of the people who were there.

NOTES ON THE TEXT

This book includes only the portions of *On Dark and Bloody Ground* relevant to the Battle of Blair Mountain and related efforts to unionize the coalfields of southern West Virginia in the 1920s and 1930s.

The original unedited audio recordings, including those of Virginia and Kentucky participants, reside at the Gelman Library at George Washington University, where I donated them in 2011. They are searchable as the Anne T. Lawrence Mine Workers Oral History Collection and are now available to researchers and the public. A portion of the collection has been digitized and transcribed. Though the entries included here have been lightly edited, they are essentially unchanged from the original manuscript. Several interviews have been cut from the original, in instances when the content did not relate specifically to labor history. Footnotes have been added where clarification seemed necessary.

A note of caution: the contents of these transcripts have not been fact-checked. As oral histories, they are a critical element to aid in our historical understanding but should always be taken in context of other documentary source material. In instances where unsubstantiated accusations of criminal activity were made, I either deleted the names of the accused, or retained them but noted that the accusations were not proven.

When conducting the interviews in 1972, I asked the individuals I spoke with for permission to use a tape recorder and to use their names in the report. Individuals were not taped if they did not give permission and were not included. In a few cases where indicated, they agreed to be recorded but asked that their real names not be used.

This text was produced in an imperfect United States, where white supremacy and racial oppression were, and are, a reality. Several of the people interviewed used a familiar but abhorrent racial slur when referring to African Americans; I have chosen to omit the word but indicate its presence.

THE INTERVIEWS

GRACE JACKSON

Eskdale, West Virginia

Fig. 1. Grace Jackson, Eskdale, WV, 1974 (*United Mine Workers Journal*, January 16–31, 1974. Used by permission.)

G race Jackson has been fighting for the rights of miners ever since, as a child, she walked along behind Mother Jones in her tours around the Cabin Creek tent colonies during the Paint Creek–Cabin Creek Strike of 1912–1913.

A widow, Grace lives alone in a small home across the creek from the town of Eskdale. She has remodeled her home herself, using only her two skillful hands, a good deal of physical strength, and a tasteful eye for the ungaudy but colorful. She has just finished redoing her bathroom, complete with new plumbing fixtures and a decor in various shades of lilac and purple. Next in line is her workroom, where she crafts quilts for a local cooperative[1]

---

1 Jackson refers to Cabin Creek Quilts, a quilting cooperative that organized skilled quilters in the Cabin Creek area of Kanawha County to band together to sell their work beyond the state's borders.

run by VISTA volunteers. "My theory," she says of her remodeling work, "is that if a person can sew and cut and measure and follow a pattern, well, that person can carpenter too."

Grace's favorite sport is fishing, often with "the boys." Lately, though, she hasn't been able to do as much of it as she would like, because the cold water aggravates the arthritis that has been plaguing those much-used hands. Grace jokes about her affliction in her usual salty language, but it bothers her.

Today is a great fishing day, and Grace has stayed home to nurse her hands. She is working on caulking up the fixtures in the bathroom when her interviewer comes by. Grace meticulously cleans off her delicate hands and fixes some biscuits for her guest. "Damn it I wish I was out fishing with Ernie," she says. But soon, after her interviewer has brought out some photographs of the old days on Cabin Creek, Grace forgets fishing, and gets to talking about her childhood.

"Those were Bill Hickok days up Cabin Creek," she says, rocking back and forth in her rocker, and toying with her poodle's leash. "You talk about Reno, Nevada. Well, this was *it*. In the days of prosperity, you know, those coal operators, they came in here and built themselves a fine hotel. I had friends that was chamber maids, they called them. They and I used to go down there together, and I'd work cleaning rooms with them for nothing just so I could get in there and see the place. The Dun Glen,[2] with a chandelier as big as two rooms. A ballroom with a floor so polished you could see your reflection in it. Imported Persian rugs, wall to wall—that was unheard of then, you know.

"And they brought in harlots by the carriage-full for them operators. Nowadays, you know, they dance topless. Well, back then, there was none of this pants stuff, they just danced *nude*.

---

2   The Dun Glen Hotel, built in the "red light" district of Southside in 1901, across the New River from the railroad town of Thurmond, was a notorious spot for drinking and gambling.

Didn't care about no religion or nothing. They say that there was no religion this side of Thurmond, nor no Sabbath either. And the gambling room! Wasn't uncommon to see five thousand dollars on the roulette wheel at one time. And if a man refused to pay up, why, they'd just shoot him in his tracks, yes, they would. Nobody would even miss him in the morning, but there he'd be, floating face down in the river. Would go by there and see them bodies floating there many a morning."

Pretty soon, Ernie comes by to see why Grace isn't out fishing with him. He drinks some and chews tobacco copiously, and he adores Grace. He comes over to see her often, even though, without fail, she cusses him out for his errant ways. He simply smiles sheepishly, and keeps on drinking and chewing, and keeps on coming back to see Grace.

Ernie starts looking at the photos too, and before long, Grace has gone to get her own photograph album, and we all come across a photo of Dirty Aunt Nellie and her disabled son.[3] Grace tells the story about Dirty Aunt Nellie often. When the tape recorder is running, the story is very tame. But when Grace feels that no machine is listening to her, she tells the story in a way that makes you realize how Nellie got her nickname.

"In 1912, they didn't have a union in here at that time. The miners were in slavery, in bondage. Many were killed all along Cabin Creek here, and some are buried in the graves here at Eskdale. They were striking for the union. The governor of the state sent in National Guards, which the union men called

---

3 Jackson's aunt was Nellie Bowles Spinelli, born ca. 1890, who married Italian coal miner Rocco "Rock" Spinelli in 1912. The couple lived at Eskdale on Cabin Creek. During the Paint Creek–Cabin Creek Strike, Nellie was one of at least three women convicted of violating the Red Men Act by the military court martial in Pratt, for interfering with the importation of strikebreakers. She was sentenced to a year in prison before she was pardoned by Governor Henry D. Hatfield, under the terms that she would never again "menace, or otherwise intimidate . . . any miner or other person who desires to work."

'yellow-dogs.'[4] The miners called them everything but a gentleman, because they was for the company, and against the men. They bodily threw the people out of their company houses, into all kinds of weather. They even threw one woman out of her house—she was a neighbor to my grandmother—who had just had a baby. It was the fall of the year, and real cold. The neighbors came around and covered her and the baby up with oil cloth—didn't have no plastic sheeting in them days—so that she wouldn't get wet in the rain.

"They searched your houses, day and night, for guns. Of course, the strikers had guns, but they were smart enough to keep their artillery hidden up in the woods. My uncle, he had a .44 pistol. He took a Sears Roebuck catalogue, which was about five inches thick, and cut a hole out of the middle of it and laid it out on top of his mother's sewing machine, right there with the .44 in the middle of it. They searched everything in the house, went into every drawer, dumped out mattresses, and everything, but they didn't find no .44 pistol. The men had to have guns, they had to protect themselves.

"Mother Jones wasn't afraid of the devil and all of his angels. And she'd come up to the head of the creek here and call out for all the men that wanted to be let out of slavery to follow her. And they did, scores of them.

"At Leewood, the company knew she was coming, and they had machines guns waiting there for her. Now, everybody was following her, women and children and everyone. When they got to Leewood, they had a cannon mounted on top of the company store. And they sent word that the miners had better turn back, because they was planning to let it loose on all of the miners and their families.

---

4 Here Jackson references the presence of West Virginia National Guard troops during martial law on Cabin Creek in 1912–1913. "Yellow dog" also refers to an employment contract common in the coalfields, which prohibited miners from joining the union.

"Well, I was just a child then, but I was in the march too. With my three uncles, my grandmother, my parents, and my five aunts. The children went too, because there were thugs all through them hills, and it wasn't safe to leave a child alone, he'd be shot in your absence. You talk about violence today, well, it wasn't nothing compared to what was going on back then.

"If one was going to die, they figured they might as well just all die together, because they weren't making no living anyway.

"Well, they arrived in Leewood. Mother Jones stood up there, and called them operators everything but a gentleman, and told them to damn well go ahead and fire that cannon, if they had the guts to do it. She even climbed up onto the roof of that store, and put her hands on the cannon, and called them everything in the book. She didn't care nothing for Christian language, because she loved the people, and hated them operators. Oh, she was a female Robin Hood if ever there was.

"Well, they didn't do a thing.

"Well, I was getting to telling you about my Aunt Nellie. At that time, they was bringing in transportations of scabs to work these mines here, so the men, who were out on strike, would starve to death. Those poor scabs, they were innocent, they didn't know nothing about the strike here. It was the companies, and the coal operators, they were the guilty ones.

"Well, there was only one way to put a stop to it. They started fighting hard. At Cabin Creek junction, they were bringing in another load. Well, the grapevine started, and it traveled fast, all the way up the creek, faster than any telephone. And by the time that train got up to Eskdale, my Aunt Nellie, and her husband, and several others, were waiting there at the depot for them. Bill Blizzard was there, he was just a young boy then.[5] My aunt was pregnant.

---

5 William H. "Bill" Blizzard later became the president of UMWA District 17's Subdistrict Two, based in St. Albans, and a leader of the 1921 miners' armed march. In 1945, he was appointed president of District 17, a position he held for ten years.

"Well, she stormed up to this man and asked him whether he was the damned bastard that was wrecking the strike and starving all these poor children, and this, that, and the other.

"Well, he yells back, 'Lady, it's none of your God-damned business what I'm doing with this trainload of men.'

"When her husband, my uncle, heard him speaking to her that way, he came up to him, and knocked him down. He was an Italian, a real big, husky fellow.[6] They'd just been married a little while, ten months or so.

"Well, the two of them got on top of this bastard. Nellie wore these real high old-timey boots, all laced up the ankle, you know. Well, she stomped him in the face, with her high heels, and tore his ears loose, and knocked his teeth out, and by the time the mine guards got over there, she had just about killed him.

"She was just a little thing, and pretty, with lovely curly red hair, and pregnant. But she could fight and cuss good enough to be a man.

"Well, they took Nellie and threw her in the bullpen. There were some twenty women thrown in one squalid room. They were malnourished—fed them just water and homemade biscuits—and the whole room was full of human waste. And the time approached for her to have her baby, and she was so weak she could barely get up off the floor.

"Well, Nellie's mother was beside herself. She went to see the governor of the state, and he wouldn't see her. And she was so mad she just stormed in right past the secretary, and right through his closed door. And she yelled at him, 'This strike will be over some day, and you will pay for it!' And he got scared and gave orders to have Nellie taken to the Charleston hospital.

"Well, the boy was born a total cripple. He lived fifty-nine years, but never did walk. His ears were loose, and his teeth were

---

6 Rocco "Rock" Spinelli, born ca. 1889, immigrated to the United States from Italy in 1908. A staunch unionist, he was involved in the Paint Creek–Cabin Creek Strike and later participated in the Battle of Blair Mountain.

deformed, and every time Nellie looked at that baby, she saw that bastard she had stomped down at the depot. He was very intelligent, but he could never walk. The state of West Virginia paid her off five hundred dollars.

"Well, there were a lot of women in here at that time that really knew how to fight. Nellie, and 'Ma' Blizzard, and Mother Jones, yes, I knew them all.

"It was these same women's men that marched down to Logan County in 1921. That time, my dad was running the man-trip on the track. We were living in a company house. We went out on strike too, and we got thrown out of our house into the tents. When the strike started, Logan didn't come out on strike.[7] Of course, the men wanted everybody to come out at once. So, the men boarded the passenger train, and the train wouldn't hold all the men, so many of them had to ride on the top of the cars. They went down there to bring the Logan miners out with them, so that they could have a strong union. It couldn't be just in one locality, it had to be a national union.

"Of course, a battle started, and a lot of men was killed on both sides.

"They couldn't pinpoint the men, but they knew they was from up Cabin Creek, and so they arrested a lot of the men from around here, and took them down to Charles Town, and threw them in prison.[8] They didn't have any evidence, but they arrested them on suspicion. Now, my uncle, that I was telling you about, he spent some time down in Charles Town prison. After so many months, maybe a year, they come to the end of it, and they couldn't get together enough evidence on them, and they let them free. But that was a small strike, in comparison to what had gone on in 1912."

---

7 Jackson likely refers to the Mingo County Strike of 1920–1922, in which Tug River miners made their first sustained bid for UMWA recognition.

8 Charles Town, in Jefferson County in the eastern panhandle of West Virginia, was the location of the trials of the men accused of wrongdoing during the Battle of Blair Mountain.

Grace is tiring of talking, and Ernie begins kidding her about his drinking habits. "Grace, you're too much God's woman," he chides.

"Well, you Ernie, you're going to burn in hell," she fires back, then gets up to put on the beans to cook down with a piece of fatback. Ernie gets up, and leaves to wander over to the local dry goods store to talk to Harry.

Grace looks down at her craftsman's hands. "Yes," she says, "they were just hillbillies, but they were pretty smart after all."

MANDY "GRANDMA" PORTER

Verdunville, West Virginia

I'm an old preacher woman myself," says Grandma Porter. "I've told my chillens many a time, and now it's my grandchillens, too, the sufferings we've been through. And it's so awful they can't nearly believe it. I do believe the good Lord, he watches over the righteous and the poor, and he listens to their cries.

"And just like he called down to Moses on the mountain and told him to take his people out of Egypt, so he looked down here, and he saw people mistreated. He seen his people with their hands frostbit and their feet naked, working on the railroad for a dollar fifty a day, and he seen the men working on the tipple so that their chillens could go to the company store at the end of the day for some beans for their dinner, and he's seen these men getting up early in the morning and walking by lantern light all the way to Dingess so that they could saw log for ten hours for a slab of bacon. Well, it was stinking all the way to heaven, and the Lord put up with it just as long as he could, and then he just caused things to happen. The union, I figure, was just a blessing from heaven.

"Back in 1919, I was living in McDowell County, and they didn't have the miners' union in there then, but my brother, Ezra Frye, was working over in Mingo, on the Tug River. Well, he was a real bold fellow, you know, and a real strong union man, and they was out to get him. One day, some men come along and started taking pictures of him, wanting to identify him later on, you know. Well, he was a brave man, and kind of funny too, and he just yelled at them and smiled, and said, come right ahead boys, I'd be happy to pose for you, and he looked right into their camera.

"Well, the next week, he was getting on the train from Huntington, and a car drove up that was filled with armed men. Just a minute, boys, he said, and he took off to his house to get his gun. But they must have taken his gun or something, because it wasn't there. He took off out of the back door and up the hill, but they shot him. The bullet hit him in the leg and splintered the bone all up and down the length of it. He never did walk the same, but it didn't stop him from organizing that union.

"They were going real strong for the union in Mingo County at that time. Mother Jones came down to help in the organizing drive. I saw her one time, in a restaurant in Logan. She was sitting there, and there was a whole row of men around her, with rifles across their laps and guns of all kinds. She wore a big, long dress, dragging the ground, and old-timey long sleeves and a little hat on her head. Well, I wasn't really scared, but things was getting hot in Mingo County at that time, and me going through there, you see, and that was scaring me, you see. She'd go up on this special train through the coalfields, and hundreds of miners would come to hear her. She'd say, 'Those coal operators can go to you-know-where'—say it right out you know!—'And you're working for nothing. Now, what are you doing that for? Just come along and join the union and they'll have to fall in and recognize you.' She would say anything you know.

"Well, they just joined in piles, you know, and they were all fired right away and put out of their houses. They moved into these tent colonies all around—in Sprigg, Nolan, Chattaroy, Goodman. I've seen rows of company houses all boarded up, and those miners living in just anything that would keep the rain off of them, tents, board houses they'd make themselves with no sides, and just about everything. I guess they just about starved. I'd take an oath to that any day.

"But over here in Logan County—I moved here in 1923—we couldn't even talk about the union. We was afraid, and didn't get it in until after it was made lawful, and Roosevelt had given us the right to organize. But we knew that we wanted it. One day, during the Hoover panic, and I think it was right after Roosevelt got elected, this man come by our house, and introduced himself, and asked if he could ask us some questions. He asked us just lots of them—how old we was, where we was born, who we married, how long we'd been married, where we worked, how much wages we got, how much we paid for our dried goods.

"Well, he just had pages of these questions, and I knew that he had to be building up to something. Then he came to his last question. 'Do you think that the union would be of any help?' he asked us. Well, then I caught on to it. He was just saying that there was no other way out for the people of Logan County than to join the union. But of course, he couldn't say that right out. So, I said, real bold and plain—it was free speech then you know—'Yes, I think the union would help our condition a whole lot.' Well, he remembered what I said, I'm sure, but that's the one piece of information that we gave him that he didn't write down on the pad of paper he had.

"Well, people just had to live, and they just had to join the union, that was all there was to do. So, when those organizers came back, after they'd found out we was all for it, I figure just about every coal miner in the county, probably in the whole U.S.A. too, joined the union. That's what I tell my chillens, you know. The people that worked for years for nothing, honey, don't forget it."

KELLY BUCHANAN

Matewan, West Virginia

When Kelly Buchanan enters a room, few people take notice. He is a slight man, well over eighty years old, and he walks with his white head bowed deeply over his cane. But when he opens his mouth to speak out—as he invariably does at the union affairs, local political rallies, and Black Lung Association meetings that he regularly attends—people sit up and listen. Kelly is a man with an oratorical style that outdoes the best traveling preacher, and a history of gripes that predates the First World War. As Kelly himself puts it, grinning a great smile, "You ain't heard nothing till you've heard it from the mouth of Kelly Buchanan."

Kelly had a lot to say about the organization of the union in Mingo County. "I was working at the Keystone Mine around 1915," he remembers, "when I first saw a paper about the union. It was put out by the miners up north in Pennsylvania and Illinois. They was working two or three days a week. We were working every day, but at starvation wages. You could go in the mines and load five or six cars of coal and couldn't come out to the company store and get enough food to feed your family till you worked another day."

Kelly remembers Sid Hatfield as a supporter of the mine workers. "When the union first came in 1920 trying to organize, Sid Hatfield was a good friend of the union. He was chief of police in Matewan. Sid had been a miner up at McCarr, Kentucky. The mayor of Matewan, Cabell C. Testerman, convinced him to become chief of police.

"It was always said around here that Sid Hatfield killed Testerman in order to get his woman. That's just a lot of propaganda. Sid Hatfield didn't kill Testerman, Albert Felts did. Felts, who was in charge of the Baldwin-Felts guards, told Mayor Testerman that he had a warrant for Sid Hatfield. The Mayor said that there was no warrant for Hatfield. Felts said it was from up in McDowell County. Testerman said, 'What's the bond?' Then Felts said he wouldn't take no bond. A couple of shots were fired, and then a .44 fired. Both Testerman and Felts were killed.

"What started it all was when they throwed them miners out of the houses at Stony Mountain Camp. They took a woman who had a baby the night before and piled her out there on a mattress. It rained for three or four hours, and the women from the camp stood out there with umbrellas over her. When the news got down here in Matewan, the people went wild."

The people of Matewan, Kelly says, knew about the battle on Blair Mountain while it was going on. "There was a man from Matewan who gathered ammunition in Williamson and everywhere he could and tried to get it over to them people. You had to go up the creek bed, there was no road, and the old bus he was driving was shot up before it got to the top of the mountain. Them Baldwin-Felts thugs got all that ammunition.

"The papers came in every day on the train, and they told the true story. We got the *Charleston Gazette* and the *Bluefield Telegraph*. One paper in particular, the *Huntington Herald*, told it like it was."

Kelly expressed his philosophy this way: "A union man is a man that will give a coal operator a fair day's work for a fair day's wages. Every good union man knows that if coal companies can't make a profit, you ain't going to have a job." He worked in the mines until 1958.

"The difference working in a nonunion mine and a union

mine was like jumping out of the fire into a cool stream of water. Everybody is your buddy and they go in singing and they come out singing. Before it was every dog eat dog. When you go into anything collectively, everybody is striving to do the same thing. That's the only way you can have peace in the coalfields."

WILLARD SMITH

Matewan, West Virginia

W illard Smith lives in a little house by the railroad tracks just outside of Matewan. He only has one eye, but he's seen many things through it in his eighty years. He likes to sit and talk about them, but not many people ever take the trouble to walk up the tracks to his house and listen to his stories.

"The news was out, they was coming to Matewan that day." It was May 19, 1920, and like almost everything else that came into Matewan, the Baldwin-Felts guards were coming into town by train. Train "fifteen" to be exact.

"We was over at the station. There was a big station here back then, and we was over there in the shed when 'fifteen' came in. 'Fifteen' come in that day, and they all commenced unloading suitcases, high-powered rifles, and lots of ammunition. There were twelve that got off there. The man who was running the hotel over on Main Street was backing them and giving them information.[1]

---

1   This is likely a reference to Charlie E. Lively, a double agent working for the coal industry, who opened up a restaurant beneath the UMWA office in Matewan and befriended many union miners, while secretly reporting on their activities to the Baldwin-Felts Detective Agency. Lively and six other Baldwin-Felts agents later shot and killed Sid Hatfield and Ed Chambers in front of the McDowell County Court House, one of the major inciting events of the Battle of Blair Mountain.

All the Baldwin-Felts guards took their suitcases and their guns and went over to the hotel to eat their dinner.

"We stayed around there, and around one o'clock they come out and got in a car with Anse Hatfield, the man who was taking them around. They went up to a coal camp on the road back of the station and throwed out about eight families. Then they come back down to town and hit the street, and they went to another camp up the hollow that belonged to the same company. There was a woman there who gave birth to a small child the night before. When they come to her, why they just picked up the mattress, the woman, and the baby and carried them all out to a rock pile next to the creek. It was raining. Everyone down in the town was a miner, and when a fellow came down and told what had happened, they just looked like they went wild. They just commenced going here and yonder and across the river and everywhere.

"After it quit raining, me and this mine foreman were walking near the tracks. Them thugs came out to catch train 'sixteen.' They come down to the station ground and went down to the post office. Next building to the post office was a hardware store. They had their guns all put together and their shotguns still buckled on, all of them did. Me and this mine foreman decided we'd go over and see what the issue was. We had to cross the tracks. They was about one hundred, maybe two hundred feet away. As soon as we got on the railroad tracks, we heard a shot fired. It wasn't five seconds between that fire and five hundred more.

"We went back into the station and Louis just hid there. I went out back and crawled under some cars. I wasn't under there by myself—I found many more. We stayed there till it quieted down. When it did, we went out and around the other end of the station. There was a fellow coming 'round the corner of the station to where we were. He had two big guns and was wearing a pair of overalls. He emptied those two guns and then filled them just as fast as anyone could. 'Bring on some more,' he hollered. 'We took care of them, we'll get the others.' Well, we hesitated about going down for a while, till we found out who he was. He was one of our men, an old fellow by the name of Ben.

"We went down and hung around a while and saw who was killed.[2] A union man and them Baldwin-Felts. We seen all of them, except for the one who was killed on the road into town. The other boys went home, but me and two more fellows stayed. We stayed around till it was pretty near dark, then we got out of there too. But man, it was dangerous out there, I'll tell you that.

"There was two thugs in our camp up there looking after us. Our boys went up there and an old fellow by the name of Butz hollered at those two, 'You fellows better be a getting your belongings. They got everyone of them that was at Matewan, and they're getting those two at Lynd.' Buddy, they got their guns and things and headed out of the camp and up the river.

"The next day they was going to put us all out of our houses. They never notified us or nothing, they was just going to throw us out. Along about one o'clock we were all setting around up there, we had nowhere to go. A fellow who was standing a hundred yards above the house yelled, 'Here comes three fellows to put us out of our houses.' They come down the road there, and we knowed every one of them. They were people raised up on Peter Creek. They come on down and went into the store. A fellow by the name of T. R. Josephs was the bookkeeper there. He fixed them up a line to start at.

"Three fellows in the camp said, 'Boys, we're up against it. We'll sleep on the ground, we'll take care of it. All of you stay in the house. Keep your kids and your wives in the house. Ain't nobody going to move nobody out of this camp.' They took their guns and went up the side of the mountain. The bookkeeper, Josephs, and the three Baldwin-Felts guards came out of the store and started to cross a wooden bridge that led to the camp. As soon as

---

2 Ten people were killed in the Battle of Matewan—seven Baldwin-Felts detectives, two miners, and Matewan Mayor Cabell Testerman.

the thugs got out onto the bridge, the fellows up on the hill were putting lead into them. Josephs ran back into the building. Them other three thugs just started running down the railroad and just kept on running."

Willard Smith doesn't see anything like that around Matewan these days. He just sits in his old rocker and watches his family grow and listens to the coal trains roll on.

HENRY
CLAY PETTRY, JR.

Lawson, West Virginia

Writing his autobiography in 1934, former UMWA District 17 Secretary Fred Mooney recalled Bill Pettry, who had successfully shared the ticket with him as the vice-presidential candidate in 1917, as "an habitual drunkard, fat, irresponsible, and prone to make grandstand plays and then pass the buck."[1]

Fred made quite a few political enemies in his day, and he may have had his reasons for being uncharitable.

Nevertheless, the record stands that on September 24, 1919, Bill Pettry was the only United Mine Worker ever to realize the collective ambition of many of the miners of his day: to deliver a bullet into the breast of the infamous Logan County Sheriff Don Chafin.

Chafin had posted bond for a man named Luther Mills, who had defaulted and escaped to Charleston. Chafin tracked him there. Mills took refuge in the headquarters of the UMWA,

---

1 The family name was variously spelled Pettry and Petry. Bill also used the last name Petry. UMWA District 17 covered southern West Virginia and parts of Ohio, Kentucky, and Virginia.

believing it to be the one place in the state the sheriff would not dare follow. He was wrong. Chafin was not easily frightened, and he collected a local deputy and charged into the union office to capture Mills.

Bill Pettry, the district's vice president, was sitting at his desk in the front room. According to newspaper accounts, at the sight of Chafin, he leaped up and yelled, "What the hell are you doing in my office!" He then reached for the revolver he habitually carried and delivered a bullet into Don's chest right below the heart.

The deputy grabbed for Pettry, jammed a gun in his stomach, disarmed him, and took him off to jail. Chafin was rushed to the hospital where gutsy fellow that he was, he recovered. The president of the Island Creek Coal Company dispatched his private railroad car to Charleston to bring him safely home to Logan.

Bill Pettry died some time ago. But his younger brother, Clay, who worshipped Bill and who, at sixteen, followed him all the way to Blair Mountain to do battle with Logan County forces led by Chafin, still lives in Lawson.

Those early years of the miners' union, those days of hard drinking, pistol-toting, hot tempers, and of men who would sacrifice all for their union, are ones which he still clearly remembers and enjoys talking about.

"Now that march on Blair Mountain," he says, sitting out on his sun porch, "I was into that. I was just sixteen at the time, and I had just started working in the mines a short time before. But I had a brother, Bill, who was into it pretty heavy, and I just got pulled into it that way, I figure.

"On April 1, 1921, we all came out on strike for a new contract on the Jacksonville [union] scale. And the operators wouldn't give us our contract, because at that time, Logan, Mingo, and McDowell Counties, those three, was running out unorganized coal, and they were selling coal on the market a lot cheaper than the organized fields could sell the coal for. Well, we were getting pretty wrought up over it, because we couldn't get no contract, and we weren't working, and they were working every day down there, and they were running out all that scab coal. That's how the whole thing got started.

"And another thing. They were terrorizing them miners down there; Sid Hatfield, they shot him down like a dog on the steps of the courthouse at Welch. And there were these miners running all over this field at the time, who had been blackballed down in the Mingo field, and they were trying to get the union started down there. Well, that's probably what really touched off the miners' fury, that killing down at Welch.

"In the first part of August, they gathered on Indian Creek, in Marmet. Well, somebody, I don't know who, was flying an observation plane overhead watching the whole thing. One thing I remember real clear, there was one fellow there, and he saw that plane, and he ran and stuck his head under a log, with all the rest of him sticking out, just as plain as could be. Well, I got a laugh out of that.

"Our plan was to go down to Logan, Mingo, and McDowell, and get those men organized. Either that or stop them from producing coal. Our aim was to get them fellows organized, and get them a contract, because then they'd get the same amount for their work we was getting for ours, and then we could all work and live. That was our goal.

"We had two passwords. One was 'I am creeping.' The other was, 'Local Union 1952—that was my local—I am creeping to Mingo.' That way, if we got halted in the woods, we could recognize each other.

"They couldn't organize that field themselves, you know. Down in that field, they had injunctions against organized labor, the coal companies did. And they had what we called thugs, wasn't anything but deputy sheriffs paid for by the coal companies. They carried pistols, and walked around in the camps, and they would beat the fellows up and club them and run them around and treat them just something awful. There was no way we could get through to these men other than having a war on our hands. These men had never worked under organized labor, and they didn't know what it was, and there was no other way we could get through to them because of all these thugs they had running all over.

"Well, the only way we was going to organize them men was to mobilize and march in there, and I mean to tell you, that's what we did, we mobilized and marched in there.

"I figure there were maybe seven hundred men in there, in Clothier, and Jeffrey, and Sharples, and Beech Creek, and Blair. To get those men in there, they took over the C&O rail train. The engine would lay over at Clothier and return the next day. Well, the miners took over the whole train, engineer, crew and all, and ran it up and down this run here, loading on men and supplies. They took a gasoline section-car, and run it along ahead of the train, and they run ahead and tell the men to get ready, the train was coming.

"I rode that train myself.

"Now, let me tell you, we was in there for business. It wasn't no cap-buster parade. And no cowboys or Indians either.

"Well, we was two weeks massing ourselves. While that was going on, Don Chafin's forces down in Logan was up digging trenches on Blair Mountain, and generally getting ready for us to come over. There was different maneuvers going on. They was getting ready for us, and we was getting ready for them, just like war maneuvers now, I figure."

Clay begins to describe the machine gun ammunition the Logan forces stocked up. It reminds him of something. He leans over, and, with an air of conspiracy, whispers, "You want to see something? Look here." He lifts his shirt and points to a long, purple scar. "*That*," he exclaims proudly, "is from one of those machine gun bullets. Just came whizzing overhead one day when I was up there on that mountain. Just missed killing me by *that* much." He pulls down his shirt and sits back. "Yes, that bullet took my cap right off. My guardian angel sure was watching over me.

"We went plumb into Logan County, to Blair, and Beech Creek. It was all one incident after another.

"Well, within a week, the soldiers come in there to disarm the miners. I was there. They came and took everybody's guns. One came up to me and said. 'Kid, what are *you* doing in this war?' Well, I may have been just sixteen, but I was mean as a snake back then, and I cussed him out, and I began to throw rocks at him. Well, I had guns, but he never did get my weapons, because I was smart and had them hid up on the mountain.

"Then, the governor sent in a C&O passenger train to bring out the miners. I lived on the Big Coal River, then, so I got off that train at Sproul and walked the rest of the way home to my dad's house.

"A week or two later, the state police come around enforcing what they called the martial law. Well, they came to my dad's house to get our guns. Well, we had a haystack, and I loaded that haystack plumb full of guns, and they didn't find a one of them. Between you and me, I was smarter than they was."

After the march had disintegrated, many miners were arrested and taken to Charles Town for trial. "They had warrants for treason against the U.S. government, and for murder, and everything else, against everyone in creation I knew about," Clay remembers.

Clay became convinced that the law was going to get him next. He took a few belongings and ran away from home. He worked his way west, riding boxcars, and got as far as Wyoming. He traveled for four years, working road gangs, picking crops in season, lumbering, and doing any other seasonal work that he could find.

When he returned finally to West Virginia in 1925, Clay was no longer the hot-headed kid who had fired his shotgun from a safe distance at Don Chafin's thugs over on Beech Creek. But he was still one hundred percent a union man. He still is.

JOHN WILBURN

Julian, West Virginia

alking about his past isn't something that comes easily to John Wilburn. In 1922, he and his father, a preacher named James, were tried in Charles Town, West Virginia, for the murder of Deputy Sheriff John Gore on Blair Mountain. They were convicted and sentenced to ten years in prison each. Their sentences were later commuted. The whole experience is clearly something that John would just as soon not remember: "There are some things," he says unambiguously, "that good Christians don't remember having happened." So, we talked about other things.

"I started working in 1919, at Omar in Logan County," John recalls. "We were all signing up for the union then at our mine. There was an organizer down there at our mine, Bill Hurt his name was, he was from the Kanawha River area, and he was doing real good, and we all thought that we had just about had all the men solid behind it and could come out for union recognition. But there was one among us, we found out later, that was a company stooge, and he pretended like he was for it too, and then, the day before we was all going to take the obligation at once, he went and told the superintendent who we all was and when we was planning to meet and all, and we all got fired right on the spot.

"Oh, it was just about impossible to get a union going in Logan then, no matter how much we was all behind it. It wasn't just these traitors, it was that Don Chafin had himself a bunch of the worst thugs you've ever seen. He kept three hundred and sixty-five gunslingers, paid for out of coal company cash, specially to break the union. I'm telling you, Al Capone in Chicago in the thirties didn't have a worse bunch than Don Chafin did at that time. You couldn't tell who was behind the union in them days, because he had everybody so scared that they didn't dare open their mouths to say a thing about it.

"Well, all of us union men that got fired, we took off and came north to get us jobs in union mines. It wasn't easy, though. They didn't want us out of the county, and we had to sneak out, all the way around through Huntington. Well, I took a job at Blair, which was in Logan County, but it was a union mine at that time. Well, I was making seven dollars a day at Blair, and I had been making four dollars a day at Omar, that's just how much difference there was at that time between the companies that was paying the District 17 scale and them that wasn't. That's why Don Chafin didn't want no miners getting the idea that they could just up and leave the county whenever they had a mind to.

"Well, Blair, you know, was right over the line that separated the union from the nonunion mines. Chafin didn't think too much of us sitting pretty over on the other side of the mountain, and every few days, he'd send a few of his deputies, Holly Smith and Billy Gore, over there to raise some trouble and run, maybe keep an eye on what was going on, you know.

"Well, one time, there was a n— man down here giving himself a big union speech to all the fellows. He had come down here from Mifflin, I think, to talk to us. Well, Holly Smith didn't like this, because he was a n— and he was talking union. He tore the clothes off that poor n—, and smashed him in the face with his gun, and dragged him off to Logan and threw him in jail. I heard the coal company this fellow worked for got angry and made them let him out. Well, it kept going on like this, they'd shoot us up a little, and we'd shoot them up a little.

"Sid Hatfield, he was the chief of police in Matewan in Mingo County, and he was real strong for organized labor. They was trying to get him out of the way. They served a warrant on him to come down to Welch. Now, Sheriff Billy Hatfield[1] offered him protection. But when he got there that day, there was no protection. As we was going up the courthouse steps there at Welch, C. E. Lively, the thug, was waiting for him, and gunned him down in cold blood, shot him down like a dog. Now, that's what raised the miners' fury more than anything.

"There were a lot of fellows running all over the coalfields then looking for jobs, that had been thrown out of work by the big Mingo County strike. And they spread the word around about the murder of Hatfield and Chambers.[2] And they started broadcasting around in mass meetings and everything what all was going on down in Mingo County, and the next thing you know, we was all fighting on Blair Mountain.

"They run a train through Blair and came down to pick us up to go fight. Just about all of us that worked there, I reckon, joined on right away. We knew that it was the only way to get them scab fields organized for good. There was a little incident over at Beech Creek, when Captain Brockus of the State Police dressed some thugs up in police uniform and tried to lead them up there to shoot up some miners. Then, the battle really got going.

"Now, a lot of people will tell you that Bill Blizzard was the leader of it all. Now, Bill's one of the finest people that's ever lived, don't get me wrong, and even though Bill and I have disagreed on lots of things, I'd vote for him if he was still living, and I was in the hospital the day he died. But he wasn't the leader any more

---

1 McDowell County Sheriff W. J. "Bill" Hatfield was a distant relative of Sid Hatfield. Welch is in McDowell County.
2 This refers to Sid Hatfield and his deputy, Ed Chambers.

than any of the rest of us was, from the way I see it. We was just all leaders, in a manner of speaking.

"I was in only one close call in the battle, most of the time it was just sniping at each other from a distance, with you never really knowing where your enemy was. I had a man raise his gun on me, and I was looking right down the muzzle of his gun, and he shot, and the same instant I dropped down, and he killed the n— behind me.[3] I'm telling you, I was scared, real scared. That was John Gore that shot at me. Well, that was the only time I come real close to anyone in the whole thing.

"But, when we found out that the government was against us too, the whole thing fell apart. General Bandholtz come in there with his troops, and he told his men not to shoot, that he wanted the whole thing done real peaceable, like, and it was done just the way he wanted. He arranged for a train to take us all home, and they just all come out real quiet, like a child taking orders from its mother. Most of those fellows was veterans of World War I, you know and there was nothing going to make them raise a gun against the U.S. Army. They would honor the orders of their government. And it stayed that way too. The union just had to wait until the government got in there behind it."

---

3 This man was likely Eli Kemp, the first union supporter killed in the Battle of Blair Mountain. Severely wounded, he was taken off the mountain and died on the operating table at a doctor's office in Blair at 11 a.m. on August 31, 1921. Little else is known about his identity.

FRANK BLIZZARD

Ohley, West Virginia.

Fig. 2. Frank Blizzard, Cabin Creek, WV, 1974 (*United Mine Workers Journal*, January 16–31, 1974. Used by permission.)

F rank Blizzard is the youngest brother of Bill Blizzard. He now runs Blizzard's Place, a bar-grocery-restaurant. He's seventy-two years old, but keeps a pistol handy behind the bar, "just in case." While we talk, he brings out the gun and loads and unloads it.

At first, he doesn't reveal much. He says he doesn't know much about the march or his brother's participation in it. Then, after a while he says, "What the hell, he's dead anyway, and they can't try him for it now." Evidently, the men had some agreement about silence, because the details of who was involved and to what extent have never been clear.

Frank was only in his teens at the time of the march. He tells the stories about Bill from the perspective of a younger brother, with clear admiration for his actions. "He was with them most of the time. He was the one that instigated it all, goddamn it, he helped them to go on. He furnished the food. He made speeches, kept them happy, cause they didn't know. He's the one that engineered the whole thing, organized them under army rules. There were plenty of smart men, just got out of the army, the rest of them, dumb as horses. Broke them down into ten-man platoons."

The reason for the march was that the southern fields were undercutting the Kanawha fields. Frank explains that Bill Blizzard and other organizers for the UMWA had tried several times to organize in Mingo and Logan Counties, but had always been driven off. The Matewan massacre was one incident in this effort.

Frank also said that District 17 officials had obtained support from Kanawha Valley coal companies, since the Kanawha fields were constantly being shut down not only by strikes but by the lower prices of coal from the southern fields. He went on to describe how the miners got their rifles from a department store owner in Charleston who was a union sympathizer. "We paid cash for them—surplus rifles, Krags, and Springfields. We'd drive up to the store and put the guns under the straw on the wagons, then drive off with the rifles."

Frank went along on the march, but because of his age, he wasn't allowed to go up on the ridges of Blair Mountain where active sharpshooting was going on. He says the march gathered men as it advanced from Marmet to Blair.

He tells a story on himself. Puffed up with pride on account of being Bill's brother, he tried to throw his weight around. He was "tried" by some of the men in a military-like tribunal for dangerous conduct and removed from the scene of the action to the rear area.

He says his whole family went along: Sarah "Mother" Blizzard, his sisters, and his brothers. After it was over, Bill was arrested and stood trial for treason against the state of West Virginia in 1922; he was acquitted.[1]

Frank feels they were winning at the time the federal troops intervened. None of the miners wanted to fight the U.S. Army, so they were disarmed and escorted out of Logan County. Without the intervention, Frank felt the "invasion" would have been successful in neutralizing the military power of Don Chafin, the coal company warlord.

He maintained that Bill Blizzard might still be alive (he died in 1955) had it not been for his refusal to have a leg removed when cancer was found. "He said he'd rather die with his leg on, and he did."

---

1 James and John Wilburn, Walter Allen, and Frank Keeney were also tried for alleged crimes related to the Battle of Blair Mountain. The Wilburns both received sentences of ten years in prison for second-degree murder, later commuted; Allen was convicted of treason but disappeared before serving his sentence; and Keeney was eventually tried and acquitted of accessory to murder.

LANA BLIZZARD HARLOW

Ohley, West Virginia

L ana Blizzard Harlow grew up one of six children in one of the strongest union families on Cabin Creek. Today, Lana lives above Ohley, on the Cabin Creek hollow road. Her house is well tended; there's a fence around it, but no animals. A calm seventy-six years old, she tries to evade being questioned. Others have come by to question her, having heard she's the sister of Bill Blizzard, the organizer of the miners' march. She doesn't want any trouble, she says, and she's tired of talking.

But she does read and enjoys the *Miner's Voice*,[1] so she consents to "tell the stories."

"It was war, they was fighting and killing, the whole time we was growing up. My daddy[2] was a strong union man, and it was known. One time, we moved to a place on the creek. They was starting to build some houses, my daddy helping. He was working in a little mine there. Well, he worked there for a while. Then they

---

1 The *Miner's Voice* was the newspaper of Miners for Democracy, the reform movement in the UMWA.

2 Harlow's father was Timothy Blizzard, from a farming family in Nicholas County. A union loyalist, Timothy had been a Knights of Labor member before the creation of the UMWA in 1890.

got to organizing. So, we had to move on, once they found out who was doing it."[3]

The stories flow into each other. Lana isn't clear about dates, but remembers the strikes of 1902–1903, 1912, and the continuing strike that began in 1919. In her stories, it seems that the warfare between the United Mine Workers, the native-born workers, the immigrants, and the companies went on constantly, despite the attempts at settlement that normally mark the beginning and end of industrial strikes. "The companies were strong," she said, "They'd post guards up at the church, tell you if you could go in or not. They'd tell you if you could catch a train. If they thought you was going somewhere, spend your money, they'd beat you up, send you back where you come from."

For a while, her father and mother operated a boarding house for miners on Cabin Creek. "They had sixty-five boarders, one time. Then he got to organizing again. So, they put a company man in as a boarder, a spy, you know. Well, they heard what was going on. They gave us twenty-four hours to get out."

There were four boys and two girls in the family. All the men worked in the mines, which helped the family survive the hard times. The family grew its own vegetables and raised its own livestock. The women did their own sewing, and the men did their own construction, so that when the hard times came, they were not dependent on the companies. "That's what kept us going, see, or we'd never had held out."

Lana's oldest brother died in the mines when he was twenty-three. Her next oldest brother worked in the mines for some time, and then became a fireman on the railroad. Then came Bill. She doesn't remember anything special about Bill, except he was a strong man, and he was honest.

---

3 For their pro-union activities, the Blizzards were evicted from their coal camp house in Kilsyth, Fayette County, during the New River Strike of 1902. They resettled on Cabin Creek and eventually purchased property at Eskdale, at the confluence of Coal Fork and Cabin Creek, where they allowed strikers to set up tents during the Paint Creek–Cabin Creek Strike of 1912–1913.

Even though the Blizzards supported John L. Lewis, Lana believes that Lewis's support of a national contract covering the entire coal industry ultimately led to the collapse of the union in the late twenties.

She also felt the miners in the "southern fields" (Logan, Mingo, and McDowell Counties) sold out during the union's attempts in the early twenties to organize them. "Of course, they had Chafin to deal with. We had one of those up here," she said—a coal company–backed "deputy" who acted as a warlord, with a commission from the coal companies for every ton of coal shipped from their fiefdoms.

Her conversation repeats the themes of union organizing, battling the operators, losing (sometimes because of "selling out"), and starting all over again. The Battle of Blair Mountain was the last of this cycle in the twenties, although after losing, she points out, Bill Blizzard kept on organizing. He died while working for District 17 in 1955.

Towards the end of the interview, her son Tom came by to see how his mother was doing. Next to his large frame, she looked quite fragile. It was difficult to equate the desperate struggles we'd been talking about with this frail grandmother. She pointed out that both she and her son had outsized jaws, which she said was the "breeding mark" of the Blizzards.

MARY PAYNE

Eskdale, West Virginia

B oth Mary Payne's husband, Bill, and her brother-in-law were part of the core group of union men from Cabin Creek who organized and led the armed march on Blair Mountain. Mary, however, felt her place was in the home and kept out of their affairs. Her memory is sporadic. It focuses briefly to illuminate a single detail here, and another there, but leaves the whole panorama in shadow.

The Battle of Blair Mountain, she thinks, was "over" somebody being killed in McDowell County.[1] She remembers more clearly the stories that her husband told her about how he was treated by Don Chafin after he had been captured on the mountain and imprisoned in the Logan County jailhouse.[2] "Don Chafin's men fed my husband plates of beans with little bits of crushed glass mixed in with them. He was so hungry, you know, that he just picked out the glass with his fingers and ate the beans real

---

1 This is likely a reference to the murder of Sid Hatfield and Ed Chambers by Baldwin-Felts agents in front of the McDowell County Court House on August 1, 1921.
2 After the Battle of Blair Mountain, hundreds of miners were indicted and imprisoned in Logan County for their alleged involvement in the conflict.

carefully afterwards. They sent guards in there to the prison to talk with him, and they hit him, and threatened him, and everything else."

Mary's brother-in-law was also captured and taken prisoner. Mary remembers that he managed, by some extraordinary ruse, to escape from the heavily guarded jailhouse. He hid out that night in the wilderness near Triadelphia. The next day, sympathetic families he met were able to get word to Bill Blizzard, who sent someone up to help him get back to Kanawha County. From there, he made his way west all the way to Rock Springs, Wyoming, in his flight from legal prosecution. He remained an exile for twenty years, but eventually returned to his home in West Virginia, where he died several years ago.

CAMDEN McDORNAN

Brushton, West Virginia

C amden McDornan grew up in Boone County in the early years of the century. He entered the mines while still a boy and worked alongside his father as a trapper[1] until he was strong enough to wield a pick and shovel himself. Since then, he has worked for numerous coal companies throughout the central part of the state. He has always been a strong union man and maintains that he has never worked in a "scab" mine, even when—as in the period between 1921 and 1933—this frequently meant choosing between that and unemployment.

Although the Boone County area, where Cam was working, was largely unionized during the teens, the men, he recalls, were not always able to stand solidly together behind their organization. "They was always trying to scare the strong union men, you know, by planting moonshine stills under their houses and then trying to arrest them on it, and things like that. Or they'd put us all out of our houses, and we'd have to move into shanty towns—'redneck towns,' they'd call them—trying to break up our union." Faced with constant intimidation by the operators, the men were not always

---

1 "Trappers" were boys hired to open and close trap doors in the mines to let mules and mining cars pass through. Trap doors were used to control ventilation.

able to stick it out. "We'd be out on a strike," he remembers, "and some of them would stay out a few days and then they'd go back to work. They'd say that they had a family to support and all."

In 1921, the message went out for all the union men to join the march on Logan County. The aim of the march, Cam explains, was to organize Logan and Mingo Counties. "The miners down there wanted it," he says, "but they kept the organizers run out of there. Why, I even heard that they burned some of them up in the big incinerator they had down there in Logan." (This story, incidentally, was one that we heard from several miners, and was apparently widely believed at the time, although we could find no written evidence that it was true.) "The operators was hollering, you know, that while we was all out on strike up here, that they was running that cheap coal out of Logan. If this side of the mountain was organized, they said, why not the other side too?"

A train—"the high-powered train, we called it, because of all the high-powered rifles on it"—was run through the area where Cam was working, and all the miners were ordered to "load on." The men weren't given much choice. "It was either load on, or hide out, I guess. One fellow, I remember, he just hid under his cabin it must have been for a week or so. No one was going to make him go up on that mountain." The majority, perhaps all, of the miners in Cam's local joined the march south.

Cam does not remember very many specific incidents of the weeklong battle. "That was, you know, an awfully long time ago." He never made it to the top of the Blair Mountain ridge, and he's not sure that any of the other miners did, either. The men were never too sure, as he remembers it, what they were supposed to be doing. "We were all pretty nervous, you know. We'd just shoot at anything that moved." At night, the men camped out in the woods in small groups. At one point, the men discovered a bomb which had been dropped by an airplane flown by Chafin's forces. It was a simple affair—"just a lot of buckshot and some powder and a fuse inside a piece of six-inch pipe"—and had failed to go off. Cam laughed about it. "It might have been," he agreed when it was suggested by his interviewer, "that the bomb maker was on our side."

The march broke up when federal troops arrived on the scene. Cam described the event. "We didn't want to surrender, but the troops was there and they said to load on, and they had a whole regiment of soldiers there, and we just all figured that we had no choice. You know, you just can't fight the U.S. Government."

AGNEW THOMAS

Sylvester, West Virginia

A gnew Thomas lives with his wife, Artie, in a comfortable house outside of Sylvester, in Boone County. They are building a house next door to rent out. Agnew got his black lung check and finally received his pension about three years ago.

Agnew and Artie have a habit of speaking at the same time. Artie broke her back in a fall and can't get out, so she enjoys visitors as much as Agnew.

Agnew says he was always a strong union man. He was secretary of his local when he retired. Both he and Artie are pro-Miller and pro-reform[1] and were active members of B-CAN, the Boone County Action Agency, an independent "people's group." They are active in anti–strip mining and support the Boone County Welfare Rights Organization.

Agnew grew up next to Paint Creek and saw Mother Jones when he was a child. "She was the cussingest woman you ever heard," he remembers. "But the miners loved her. They'd do what she said."

Agnew started working in the mines when he was sixteen.

---

1 This refers to Arnold Miller and to the Miners for Democracy, the movement to reform the UMWA on whose ticket Miller ran for the presidency of the union.

When he was eighteen, Agnew heard there was trouble down in Logan, got his rifle, and he and a few friends went off to join the marchers. Word got back to his parents that he'd been killed. His father went down to pick up his body, but found Agnew alive and well, working for one of the cooks. Shooting was still going on, and his father convinced him to come home to show the relatives he was all right. They walked into the wake being held for him. By the time he thought about going back to the fight, it was over.

Agnew believes that the march on Logan was the result of an agreement between the union leaders and the Kanawha County coal operators. He cites as evidence the fact that he received his rifle from the company store, on credit, at a time when no one had worked for a long time. Further, he says, if "they" had wanted to stop the march, they could have called in the federal troops or the National Guard long before the marchers reached Logan County.

He wasn't allowed up on the ridge and doesn't remember the marchers being as organized as Frank Blizzard recalled, although he confirms that William Payne was the "general" in charge.

He said that he felt one reason for the failure of the march was that the miners in Logan didn't want to be unionized. The march "broke the union," he thought, by revealing its inability to unionize the southern fields. However, in 1933, the miners there accepted the union when it became legal and "Chafin wasn't around anymore. Before that, it was too hard. They'd as soon kill you as talk to you, that's all they thought about human life."

Most of Agnew's old buddies left the area during the years after the march failed, and the Depression began. During the Depression, Agnew "worked in the mines when I could, rest of the time, I worked on our farm. We fed many a man, couldn't fill his bowl, come in looking for a job."

He remembers the march as an adventure. "We didn't know what was going on, then. Since then, I thought about it, figured it out. Then, we went for the adventure. To tell the truth, I think most of the men went for that."

ELBERT GORE

Holden, West Virginia

I t has been just over fifty years[1] since union miners from all through northern West Virginia converged on Blair Mountain to do battle with the infamous union-busting sheriff Don Chafin and his army of deputies in their attempt to organize the Logan County coalfields. Many eyewitnesses have died, and many memories have lapsed.

Every man and woman who was living in 1921, however, seems even today to remember one incident in the weeklong battle. Perhaps it was because it was widely covered in the Logan newspapers. Perhaps because, for many people, it seemed to demonstrate conclusively the deadly seriousness of the conflict. Perhaps because it was the first time in Logan's history that the sheriff and his retinue were revealed to be vulnerable. Or perhaps it was because two major trials resulted.

On August 31, 1921, while patrolling Blair Mountain for signs of unionists on the march, Don Chafin's chief deputy, John Gore, was shot and killed by union miners. It was the first, and for some, the most tragic casualty of the battle.

---

1 As of the date of the interview, 1972.

Many people remember that death, even today. Perhaps none of them remember as vividly as Elbert Gore, John's son.

"At the time of the miner's march, I was a schoolteacher," Elbert remembered. "I taught up at Sharples, up the creek there; and that was where a lot of the fighting and trouble was. I was living up there with my mother and brother and sisters. We were living over there on a farm, on the Blair side of the mountain. All my relatives were deputy sheriffs. My dad was a deputy sheriff, and two of my brothers was deputy sheriffs, and my uncles was deputy sheriffs. My dad, he was a deputy sheriff. He stayed over at Ethel, on this side of the mountain.

"The miners over there at Sharples got suspicious of me. All his people are deputies under Don Chafin, they thought, and he goes over to Logan about every weekend. So, in the little schoolhouse where I was teaching, I went over there one morning, and written on the blackboard, in great big letters, was: *ELBERT GORE. BALDWIN-FELTS DETECTIVE.*

"And another time, it was on Sunday. I went to Sunday school that morning, and they announced that the church service would be in the afternoon. I went down, intended to go to the church service. There was no women or children there, just a bunch of miners. I thought, well, they're having a union meeting. I'll just sit down out here, under a tree, and wait until it's over. So, here directly came three or four of them, and said, 'Gore, you're going to have to leave. We can't have you hanging around here. We're having an important union meeting.' I said, 'Well, I intended to go to church.' 'There's not going to be any church service,' they said. I said, 'All right boys, I'll see you later.'

"It was more or less a tradition in my family to be a sheriff. My grandfather's brother was sheriff back in the nineties. My dad became deputy sheriff back in 1912, when Don Chafin was first elected sheriff of Logan County. And, he was the reason that his brothers and his sons and all of them followed him into law enforcement, too. I was deputy sheriff from April 1942 until September 1966. I was deputy sheriff for twenty-four years and six months. I claim that I served as deputy sheriff for longer than any other man in Logan County.

"Now, at that time, the sheriff's office was used mostly to fight the union. But it wasn't always that way. Logan's always had a sheriff to enforce the laws and collect taxes. The purpose of the sheriff's office is not to fight the union. But Logan County, like a lot of other counties, was a small and poor county, and they—the taxpayers—couldn't pay for the proper law enforcement, or the number of officers they needed to enforce the law in the county after the coal companies started coming in here.

"Back when these coal mines were first started, there weren't many people living around here, and most of them didn't know anything about coal mining. They were timber men or farmers. So, in some of these big coal camps, like Holden, the county couldn't pay for a deputy sheriff, or two, or three, to live here in Holden and patrol the coal company's property. So, the coal companies said, well, we'll pay it. And so, they started paying the officers, or constables, whatever they was called. Most of them was called deputy sheriffs. Of course, they had pistol licenses, to carry pistols. And, they were deputy sheriffs, but they was paid for by the coal companies, instead of by the taxpayers.

"Later on, then, when they started sending organizers in here to organize the coal miners, why, of course, the coal companies gave these deputies orders to keep them out, and not to let them come in there. And that's how they got tied up like that, originally. When Don was sheriff, now, the coal companies would pay the deputies part of their salary, and Don would pay them part of it. But they got to having so much trouble, and so many organizers come in here, that Don made the coal operators pay by the tonnage to pay the deputy sheriffs. And to buy guns in case of emergency, and things like that.

"Now, Kanawha County had a lot of coal, produced nearly as much as Logan and McDowell and Mingo. And, of course, the union heads, the officials of the union, said, 'If we can get those counties organized, and those union dues will make us rich.'

So, they tried their best to organize. It would mean more miners paying dues to them, you see. That's how this miners' march started.

"Well, once in a while you'd find Logan County miners that was for the union. Probably the biggest part of them wanted to join the union. But they didn't OK the forcible joining. They didn't want any of that. And that's what Keeney and Mooney came to do, to force it on them, to make them join. So, between one side and the other, wasn't much difference. So, they fought for Don Chafin. There was hundreds of them. Don and the coal operators furnished the guns. They had the guns already, bought up from this royalty. They already had plenty.

"So, Don just sent out a call, when the miners started to march towards Blair Mountain, for volunteers, and hundreds of coal miners went to Logan, and were sworn in as deputies or special deputies, so that they could lawfully carry guns. Well, some of them were killed over at Blair Mountain. Two of them were killed with my father.

"Now, it wasn't exactly the union that they was fighting against, it was the way that the union was trying to force unionism on them. That was the argument, mostly. They made brags, those miners from Paint Creek and Cabin Creek, that they was going to hang Don Chafin and burn the courthouse down, and tear up all the coal tipples, blow them off of the map, and all that. Well, the coal miners that had families over here, they didn't want any of that.

"Captain Brockus was head of the state police at the time, in Williamson. He brought forty or fifty state police to Logan on August 27, and asked Don to give him some deputies to go serve these warrants over at Beech Creek. I was at home, there on Beech Creek, and I heard them people go down the road. I had an uncle or two was in it, and an older brother was in it. They were deputy sheriffs.

"I heard them going down the railroad tracks, right across the creek. I didn't have an idea what it was, didn't give it any thought. Until a few minutes later, I heard a lot of shooting, right down below where I lived. And, directly here came men up the road, some on one side of the creek, some on the other. As they went down now, they were all kind of in line, were not smoking a cigarette, and not talking. Quiet. They went down there and run into this bunch of union miners that tried to stop them. And when the shooting started, of course, Captain Brockus gave all his men orders to fall flat on the ground. To keep from shooting each other. But in the dark, they all got scattered. They weren't properly organized. Some went one way, some another.

"So, next morning I heard what had happened. They had gone down to Mifflin, down below Sharples, and there was a bunch of miners there, sixty or seventy of them, with guns. And they disarmed these deputies and state police, and took their guns off of them, and told the state police to leave. They just had been there at Sharples a couple of days. And the miners run them off and disarmed them.

"So, Governor Morgan gave Captain Brockus orders to get warrants and go over there and arrest them. So, Captain Brockus got the warrants, and got thirty or forty state police with him, and came to Logan, and got these deputies, and went over there to serve the warrants. Of course, that was a bad thing to do, was inviting trouble. That was the spark that set off the miners' war. Of course, it had been brewing all along. But that was the spark that touched it off.

"He went over there to serve the warrants, and that was when the trouble happened. The men, they were out patrolling the roads, the miners were, over there. I don't know whether they were expecting something like that over there or not. But they were prepared for it, and they stopped Captain Brockus and his contingent of state police and deputies and fired at them. So, of course, they fired back, and killed three of them, Captain Brockus and his men. Of course, no one knows who exactly fired the actual shots. They had to disperse then, because they figured that if there was a gang there, that all the way down the road they'd be running into them. And have some of his own men killed and kill a lot more of them. So, they just came back. Came back to Logan. But they didn't come back like they went down. Came back talking, whistling, laughing. But when they went down now, they was just as still, quiet.

"So, knowing that they suspected me, that morning when I heard about it, I had a friend lived right up above me, and his brother was a deputy sheriff over there too. And he was afraid that they suspected him. He and I started to Logan. And we had to go through the woods, we couldn't follow the highway, because they'd stop us, arrest us. We went through the woods and worked our way over the mountain. We knew that we wouldn't come across the mountain directly to Logan, we'd have to come in a roundabout way. So, we went over to Hewett Creek. I had an aunt lived over there. And me and this fellow, just about daylight, we came off of the mountain. We hadn't had anything to eat since the morning before. We went into my aunt's house.

"While we were in there, somebody had seen me there, a boy that she had raised. He had gone out and told that we were there. While I was eating, I looked out, and all around the house were miners with rifles and guns. So, two of them came in and said, 'Gore, you'll have to go with us.' I said, 'Well, why? What's the trouble?' 'Well, they think you're a Baldwin-Felts Detective.' I went with them.

"The day before, they had caught these other four fellows that had got lost that night. Fult Mitchell and Lucian Mitchell and two others.[2] And they had them over on Hewett, at a farmhouse. And when they arrested me, they took me down to this place. But they had already moved these four from there by then.

One said, 'let's take him and put him with these other four thugs.' And Lewis White—I knew him, he was one of the leaders of the miners—he said, 'no, we won't do that.' We don't have any

---

2 According to later trial testimony, the four men were Fulton Mitchell, Lucian Mitchell, Howard Young, and Leslie Stanley.

handcuffs to put on this boy. If he started running, or something, and something happened to him, we'd have to kill all of them, to leave no witnesses.' And he said, 'We don't want them together.' And so, they took me down to Jeffrey. There was an old fellow down there, supposed to be a preacher. But they'd tried—he told me—to make him go with them, but he'd talked them out of it, because he was kind of old. So, they had said to him, 'We'll give you a job. You can just keep this fellow under guard until this thing is over.' Well, I stayed over there.

"He treated me good, except everybody would come along, and he'd come back in. He'd say, 'Oh, I hate to tell you Elbert, but things are looking bad for your outfit over in Logan.' And then when my dad was killed, of course, well, he came and told me about that. My dad was killed on the thirty-first of August. They had me prisoner over there. He was buried, of course, but I couldn't come to his funeral. He was buried before the soldiers came in and released me. They kept me prisoner for about five days, until the United States soldiers came in.

"I guess that that was the closest the two sides ever got together, was when my father was killed. Mostly, they just fired at each other at long range. Of course, both sides had a password. The defenders, Don Chafin and his deputies, had "AMEN." The others had "COME CREEPIN."

"The night my father was killed, it was right foggy, early in the morning. And this group of miners came around the high place on the top of the mountain. And he thought that it was some of his own men, my dad did. So, one of the fellows he was with, said, 'John, that's not our men, let's shoot!' Dad said, 'No, let's be sure. I'd rather be killed myself than kill some of my own men.' And they got right up, right close to each other. And I reckon my dad saw his mistake then. He hollered, 'Give me your password!' But it was too late.

"A colored from up at Ethel, a coal miner, he wasn't with him at the time, but he come back off the mountain and reported that my dad was killed. And some of them said, now, you sure about that, Hossie? Hossie was the Black man. He said, 'Yes, I'm sure. I crawled up and laid my hand on him, and shook him, and spoke to him.' He said, he didn't move. Well, he evidently had his gun raised, his rifle, when he was asking them for their password. But before he could shoot his gun, the bullet had hit the rifle, split the stalk of the rifle, and had gone square through him. He fell, of course, and they ganged up around him then. One of them put his rifle right down to his forehead and fired again.

"They were dangerous times, back then."

OCTAVIA YOUNG

Holden, West Virginia

I n 1921, Howard Young was working for Don Chafin as a traffic officer. Although he was not himself one of Chafin's chief deputies, these men were his closest friends. "Bill Gore, he was one of the main deputies, and his brother, and a whole bunch of them, and Howard, they all used to run together," recalls Howard's widow, Octavia. "We come here to Logan in 1914," she continues, "and Howard worked a couple of years in the mines, but he quit to take work as a cop.

"The work was mostly routine. But one time, I remember, Howard came home all bloodied up because of a fight he'd been in with somebody in one of the camps. When it would get that bad, they'd just call a J.P.[1] and have a trial right then and there."

According to one version of the story, Howard was with a group of men who were sent up Beech Creek on a patrol shortly after hostilities broke out on Blair Mountain. The men spent the night moving up the creek bed, then stopped to rest at the home of a friendly farmer, and unwisely left their rifles propped up outside on the porch. A group of union men, led by Bad Lewis White, saw them, surrounded the house, and took the men prisoner. The

---

1 Justice of the Peace.

miners wanted to kill the deputies immediately, but Bad Lewis held them back. They say that Chafin later returned the favor when Bad Lewis was picked up on the streets of Logan.

Octavia was in the hospital in Logan at the time of the battle giving birth to the couple's first son. But she was not totally removed from the situation. That year, she had been up to visit relatives on the Kanawha River several times. "Their youngest boy," she says, "He was a real hot-headed radical. He'd talk real big all the time, about what he was going to do, how he was going to come down here and 'clean up' the place. You'd think, from the way he was talking, that Don Chafin had horns or something. So, I had some idea of what they was planning to do.

"Now, I don't have too much remembrance of what actually went on on the mountain, but I do know that they were about to kill Howard, and some man stopped them. Now, I don't know what his name was, but I do know that he had been dating the girl that was working for us at the time that the baby was born.

"Actually, you know, they didn't tell me that Howard had been captured until afterwards, because they didn't want to upset me. But I don't know what hurt me more, that, or his not coming to see the baby until eight days after it was born! It was our first, and we had waited for it for eight years."

GEORGE SWAIN

Charleston, West Virginia.

Fig. 3. George Swain, Charleston, WV, 1974 (*United Mine Workers Journal*, January 16–31, 1974. Used by permission.)

T oday, boys go into the service and get a chance to travel around a lot when they're still young," George Swain says.[1] "Things were different when I was growing up. I don't claim to have traveled very much. But the little town of Norris, Kentucky, where I grew up, it was just about God's paradise to me. That's where I had my first romance, and where I got my first job, picking potatoes and cutting corn for thirty-seven and a half cents a day. We sure had to work for what we got back in them days.

"When I came to West Virginia, I found work on the tipple. I made a dollar, a dollar and a half, a day. That was paying so little that pretty soon I went inside the mine to work, driving a mule

---

1 Swain is the author of *The Blair Mountain War: Battle of the Rednecks*, originally published in 1927, which gave an anti-union account of the battle from the coal operators' perspective.

and hauling coal, and I went from there to working on the cutting machine. Then I got a job bossing over at Omar for the Main Island Creek Coal Company and bossed a gang of men working in the mines. We all got along fine, white, colored, Italian, what have you. That's how I went from trapper to boss in the mines.

"The story of how that mine got started is pretty interesting, if you've a mind to hear it. There was a fellow named Jack Dalton, worked as a superintendent over in Elkhorn, Kentucky. Well, he heard about these beautiful unused mountains over here at the head of the Guyandotte, and he loaded him up a mule—weren't no roads across the mountains in them days—and came across the mountain to Logan. He was a big man, and didn't have no education hardly, could hardly even write his name. Well, he met up with a young lawyer, a real brilliant young fellow, and the two of them decided to go in it together.

"Well, the first problem they had was getting the land. The land around here was all leased out to Cole and Crane, the saw-loggers. So, they took up to Charleston and called on Old Man Laing, the state superintendent of mines,[2] and persuaded him to go with them over to Cincinnati to try to lease some of the land off'n Cole and Crane. Well, they said they could have some land to open up a mine, but they'd have to put six thousand dollars down. Well, neither of them boys had any money at all. So, they went out in the hall and conferred. Dalton, scratched his head and said, 'Look, I have a sister who works as a teacher over in Virginia, and she's got some savings.' So, they came back into the room, and wrote out a check for six thousand dollars, and forged her name to it.

"Well, they commenced making money hand over fist. The First World War started, and the orders for coal were really pouring in, and they were real clever and set up offices all over, and one of their agents would sell to another, and that way they could make up to seven dollars on a ton of coal, even though the government

---

2 John Laing was a successful Scottish coal operator in southern West Virginia who became the chief of the Department of Mines of West Virginia in 1908.

at that time had put on a price ceiling of three fifty. It wasn't long before the Island Creek Coal Company offered them no less than twelve million to buy out their mines. But of course, by then they just thought they were never going to stop making money, and they refused to sell out.

"Well, two years later, they sold their property for four thousand dollars, which just about covered their closing expenses. That's when the bottom plumb fell out of the coal industry.

"I became very friendly, during those years I was bossing at Omar, real intimate, you might say, with Don Chafin. Boy, he did a lot for me, just a whole lot.

"Now, at that time, the union was sending organizers down here in the Logan field. There weren't any roads down here then, and the only way into the county was by train. Well, Don had deputies at the station, and they watched to see who would get off the train, and if anyone looked suspicious to them, they'd just tell him right then and there, 'Buddy, you can catch the next train out.' Or they made them walk out, I guess.

"You've probably heard about the time Mother Jones sent two organizers down here, and they took rooms in Don's house. When they found them out, boy did they run them out of the county fast! Don took them up to Blair Mountain ridge personally, in his automobile. John Gore, his chief deputy, I knew him real well too, was with them at the time. Well, Don wanted to kill the two of them right there, I think. But Gore, he restrained him, and said, 'Don, you can pistol-whip them if you want, but I don't think it would be a very good idea to kill them.' Well, those two fellows were lucky they made it out of there alive.

"Don Chafin had a secret service. In fact, I worked for him for a while as a secret service agent. I'd listen around at my mine and see if any of my boys were talking about striking or anything like that. We'd record it if they did, and the mine owner would fire them right quick. We never said that that was the reason though, we'd always say that it was that they had missed a day, or that their work wasn't of a very good quality, or something like that.

"Our miners were all happy. Our men were well paid, not quite as well as in the union mines, but almost as well. And they lived in good little houses that the company built. And there were lots of jobs to be had in that field. I never heard of no discontent, or anything like that.

"Logan miners were satisfied, for this reason: they knew they'd have to be out part of their wages if they joined the union, that they'd have to give it up for union dues. And so, they were satisfied how things were run.

"And another thing, there wasn't nothing we wouldn't do for a man, if he was a hard worker and didn't make no trouble. If they were good workers, they could go to the paymaster and draw up to a hundred dollars in advance with no questions asked.

"Now, I remember one man that came in from St. Louis on transportation. I was the only company man he had met when he first got in, and a few days after he had arrived, he come to me and asked if I could do a favor for him. 'Sure,' I said, 'if I can.' 'Well,' he said, 'I had to pawn my watch in St. Louis to get the money to come down here. It was a real good gold watch, and I need it, and the time is about to run out on it. Can you send the money for it, and I'll pay you for it as soon as I can work it off.' Well, I went to the paymaster, and took the money, and sent for that watch. When it come in, I called the fellow into my office. He was a little scared when he come in, I think, thinking that I had heard someone hearing him talking, or something like that. 'Harry, here's your watch,' I said. 'But I don't have the money yet to pay you,' he protested. 'Well, I took a look at your work record,' I said, 'and your record has just paid for your watch.' Well, it wasn't long after that that we had him working for us as a superintendent, and he made a darned good one too.

"During World War I, labor was so scarce that Jack Dalton used to run trainloads of workers in there from all over—Kentucky, Texas, everywhere. Transportations, we called them. One of my jobs was to take their names down and get them started when they first come in there that way. One night, a train came in. We was really busy getting things ready for them, cooking up food in big vats, laying out mattresses in a big hall for them to sleep on, and everything else getting prepared. Well, a hundred and thirty men come in that night. But forty escaped into the woods that night. They knew they'd be charged for their transportation against their first paycheck, and they went off to find work at other mines where they wasn't known.

"Well, we got alcoholics, and tramps, and everything else, but we did get some very fine coal loaders come in that way. One man, I remember, was real scared when I first talked to him. 'Isn't there any work you can give me on the tipple?' he said. 'I've never seen a coal mine in my life, and I'm afraid to go inside.' So, I assigned him to be the plumber's assistant. And he made the best plumber's assistant we've ever had. He left after one year, and took the money he had saved, and went back up to Cincinnati, I think, to start his own business.

"Another incident I can remember might interest you. It was also my job to take care of those boys when they got hurt. The company retained two doctors over there at Omar. One day, I got a call that they were bringing a man down out of the number six mine. That was about a half mile up the creek. Well, I went and got the doctor, and we took off, and met them just as they was bringing this boy down off the mountain in a stretcher. He was only about seventeen years old. We leaned over to see how bad he was hurt. He was moaning real soft, 'It's my hip, my hip.' We packed him into the coal train and run him into Logan to the hospital. An hour later, I got a call that he was dead. I wired his family if I should ship the body, but they wired back that they didn't have any money, and that we should bury him up here. Well, you'd be amazed how many of them boys turned out to follow the casket up the hill to the burying ground.

"The boys were all like that. It was a funny thing, even if they didn't know each other personally, they would always come to another fellow's burial. And if a man was sick or hurt, the first thing you'd know, one fellow would be passing around the hat for the benefit of John Jones, or whoever, and wasn't one of them that wouldn't put something in it.

"Well, the very next day, I remember, was another man hurt in the mine. But this one didn't die. I could hear him squalling about half a mile away when they carried him out of the mine, but he was lucky. They only had to cut off part of his big toe.

"I don't know. Maybe this doesn't interest you at all. But these are just the little incidents that stand out in my memory of life there at the Omar mines.

"I never knew of any bathhouses there at Omar. Sometimes, though, the men would fix themselves up a little shower bath or something like that outside of the mine. Then, after they'd washed up, they'd go out to the pool rooms, or just go visiting among themselves. Just needed someone to talk to. That was one thing about them miners. Had to have some communications.

"Do you know what a trapper boy is? They used to hire little boys to open and shut the doors in the mine when the mule cars come through. Well, they had nothing to do but just sit around in there, and they'd study up all kinds of mischievousness. Right near where one little fellow worked there was a real steady drip of pure water from the ceiling. The men came along there and had set up an empty powder keg on a shelf of coal below to catch the drip. These miners would come out of the loading rooms, all hot and thirsty, and they'd use that keg for drinking water.

"Well, this little trapper decided he was going to have himself some fun. So, he got himself some wire, and put one end in the water and hooked the other end to the live trolley wire. Well, the first miner came out of loading room came over to take a drink, and I'm telling you, when his mouth hit that water he was thrown just about clear all the way across the opening.

"You'd be amazed the number of things those fellows could think up to amuse themselves and tricks to play on another miner. And then they'd laugh about it for days. But one thing they never did joke about, and that was getting hurt. You just never heard a man joke about needing help. If he hollered that he was hurt, he meant it.

"A lot of the miners we brought in here on transportation was foreigners. There was one fellow I remember very vividly. He was a Hungarian. He came to me when he first got here and asked if there was a single room in the company boarding house that I could rent him. Well, I didn't have a single, but I had a two-room apartment on the second floor in the n— section, and he said he wouldn't mind that. One time when I was going around inspecting the houses, he gave me some of his homemade wine, and it was some of the best I've ever tasted. Well, one day, I ran into a n— woman in the company store. 'Mr. Swain,' she says to me, 'do you know anything about this here Hungarian fellow?' 'No, why?' I says. 'Well,' she says, 'I live down below him, and I'm worried, because I haven't heard anything from him, and I went up to check, and his door is locked from the inside.'

"So, Fult Mitchell, one of the deputies, and I went up there to check it out. Sure enough, the place was locked up, and we banged and hollered and hooped, but there wasn't no answer, so finally we went and knocked the door down. Well, that Hungarian was sitting there in a chair, leaned over the pine table he had built himself, dead as a doornail. On the table was a bottle, half full. We took a whiff of it. It was the most foul stuff I've ever smelled. Someone must have sold it to him for moonshine, but it was almost pure alcohol, and must have just poisoned him. Yes, every night there was moonshiners in that camp selling their brew.

"Most of them foreigners stayed to themselves. And the coloreds, too. But those n—s were good people. It was amazing, too, how they'd take care of themselves. Of course, if they didn't, they'd be smacked down real quick. There were a few of them colored that kind of took charge themselves of policing the n— camp, you know. If they found one of their kind drunk on the street or something, you know, they'd take him in charge and take him home. They looked after their own race pretty much.

"Well, in 1913, I went from Omar to Ethel, and from there, in 1920, I moved to Logan and got a job as a reporter on the *Logan Banner*. That's where I was working when they had all this trouble over on Blair Mountain.

"I think what started it all was that these outsiders come in there in the Kanawha fields and told them all sorts of stories about how the miners was suffering in Logan and Mingo. Told them all sorts of lies. I read that in the daily newspapers, the *Herald Dispatch* and the *Gazette*, and I understand the miners who were tried later in Charles Town even admitted to it.

"Well, the coal operators in Logan gave Don the money, and he had guns shipped in from Kentucky to defend the county. They had good guns, thirty caliber Smith & Wessons, and high-powers. And they opened up a commissary there in Logan to dispense them.

"Now, I was just a little fellow at the time, weighed only about 125. They tried to recruit me to fly the plane that flew over and dropped the bombs on the miners. But I wouldn't do that. I don't think that I'm more of a coward than other people, but I didn't want to go up there on the mountain and fight, either. Not only were there miners up there shooting at you, but you were in danger too from your own men. They had boys all over that mountain that had no idea how to handle a gun, and actually you were more likely to be shot in the back by your own troops than you were by the opposition.

"Well, I had to do something for Don, so I went to work in the commissary where they dispensed all the weapons. I had orders to give out these guns to anyone that came in and said that he was going up on the mountain to fight. Now, all of those guns were supposed to be returned after the fighting was over, but I don't think that there was a single one returned. I took two for my own use, too, and even I kept them.

"The first mistake that the Logan side made was when Brockus took those state troopers up Beech Creek near Sharples on the twenty-seventh of August. Now, I understood that the miners had been persuaded to go home at that point, and there was a train all ready to take them back. But Brockus made the mistake of charging up that creek with all those big egotistical men of his, and he should have known that he was walking into a hornet's nest. Passions were inflamed there. They were asking for it, and they got it too. Well, when the miners heard about that, they just all got off that train and came right back and started the battle all over again.

"Yes, both sides made a lot of mistakes, and neither can be called blameless.

"Now, I've got to admit I had some admiration for Frank Keeney, the president of District 17. He didn't have no education, but when he spoke, people would really listen. I visited the three of them, Keeney, Mooney, and Blizzard, when they was in the jail down here in Logan. Everyone came to see them, just like animals in the circus. Well, that Bill Blizzard, he really was a nervy son of a gun, more than the other two. When I got down there, he just struck both his hands through the bars of the jail and said real loud, 'Well, I'm Bill Blizzard, who are you?' You could see he was a regular devil. He didn't do the union too much good, because he was too radical. He was the one that urged them on, you know. But Don had instructed me and all the rest that got to see them, you know, not to show any animosity towards them, and I didn't. Don treated them pretty good, generally speaking.

"When those troops come in, both sides got out right quick. Overnight, it seemed like, both sides just plain disappeared.

"Well, after the whole thing was over, they had a display in Logan of the bodies of two of the union men who had been killed on the mountain. Well, both had just little holes in their breasts, where the bullets had entered. But if you turned them over, there were holes big enough to put your fist through. They were the only two sons of a widow woman up on Coal River. Well, that's where you could only cry. I admit it, I cried over that. Two young men, in the bloom of health, senselessly and violently dead. That's when I felt that the whole thing had been a real tragedy."

MARY GHIZ

Logan, West Virginia

Mary Ghiz's father came to Logan County in 1904 from Hungary. An older brother had come over to the States first and had written that "business was good in Logan County, West Virginia." So, John Ghiz had come, with his family. Mary was born four years later.

When he arrived, John Ghiz had to find work. He wanted to become a peddler. He soon discovered that no one could do anything in Logan County without the express permission of Sheriff Chafin. Fortunately, Chafin took a liking to the man and signed papers giving him permission to travel around as a peddler. Not all who asked him for such favors were so lucky; as Ghiz was to learn, possession of these papers was a rare privilege.

"One day," Mary remembers, "our father was out on the road peddling his dresses and material and things. He was just getting off the train—the first train they had in Logan, the one that ran down to Holden—and a strange man came up to him. 'Do you have papers from the Sheriff?' the man asked. 'I do,' said my father. He thought, you know, that the man was checking him. But when he turned to get off the train, the man followed him and put a bullet through his back. He fell but didn't die. It took them a year before they could find the bullet in his back."

Later, John Ghiz became Logan's first confectioner, and made his own candies to sell to the growing town's population of coal operators and professionals. But he still had to leave town on business sometimes. When he did, his wife and children were "scared to death," Mary recalls, until he came home, even though they were lucky enough to live in a big home on Dingess Street. "One time, the people that was against the union, it must have been, came and put machine guns, lined them up, across from our house. They was going to kill people if they caused trouble. Finally, my father got home. When he knocked on the door, my mother was scared to death. 'Who's there?' she said. 'It's just me,' said my father. She thought, you know, that it was someone that had come to kill us all before he got back."

DEWEY BROWNING

Switzer, West Virginia

"Oh, I knew about all them old boys back in Logan County in them days, on both sides," Dewey Browning remembers. "Now, I was always a miner, and a good union man, and all my kin was too. But I worked some for Don Chafin, getting out the vote, you know. So, his boys didn't ever bother me, even before we was organized in here. Lee Belcher, that was one of Don's deputies, why, he'd pass me in the road and say, 'Dewey, you seen any rednecks today?' and I'd just say, 'Only just one,' and we'd both laugh, a private little joke between the two of us.

"I always did want to be a member of the UMWA. When I was just thirteen, I used to come down to the mine after school and work for 25 cents a day drying sand. Sand to keep the cars from slipping on the track. Well, the pay wasn't nothing, but I was just a kid, liked to be around those motors. Well, the next year, I quit school for good, and went to work coupling cars, and then got to braking.

"There was a bunch of us fellows that used to sit around outside the drift mouth when we wasn't working, and one of them, an older guy it was, got to talking sometimes about how they was organized up north and how you got better wages and better hours and all, at these union mines. Well, I wasn't getting nothing for

76

my work, so one day my cousin, Reece, and I just got ourselves up and got on the train to Ethel, and then walked over the ridge to Blair. That was a long trip, then, because there was no way over the mountain. Today, you know, it just takes about thirty minutes in your car, but it took us about all day.

"Well, we spent the night with my uncle Ark and then went on down to the mine the next morning. They told me that they needed a brakeman, and I told them I could brake pretty good. 'You look awful young,' they told me. 'Well, I can work like a man, you just give me a try and I'll show you.' Well, from then on, I did work as a man. Now, that was the first union mine I worked at.

"Now, Reece and I, we hadn't been working at that mine very long when it comes time to strike. These boys was looking to get themselves a new contract. Things were getting pretty rough around there. Keeney and Mooney came down to speak to them, and they were getting wrought up, and it looked to me as if we was going to have a war on our hands.

"Well, I was still pretty young, and I wasn't for violence too much. I was a union man, but I didn't want no shooting or killing. So, I went back home to Omar. But I soon found out things weren't too much better over there. Don Chafin and his boys were coming around beating the bushes and getting everyone rousted out to fight. It was just fight, or go to jail, that was about all there was to it.

"Well, I was in a real fix. So, I thought me up a smart trick. I went on into Logan and made like I was planning on going up there to fight them rednecks, and that I wanted a pistol and a high-powered rifle, too, to do the job. But, instead of taking them guns up on the mountain, I went on back to Cow Creek, where my people was at. On the way back, I run into one of Don's deputies. And he says to me 'Dewey, where are you going with them guns? You should be up on the mountain.' And I answered, 'Don appointed me the official guard for this camp.' 'Oh, go ahead,' he says. Well, there weren't no telephones in those days, and Don didn't find out until all the trouble was over what I had been up to. Now, I kept them guns, too. Told him I had lost them down the river, and he didn't say nothing, but he probably knew. Almost killed my brother with one of them, playing around later on. Near scared me to death.

"Well, like I was telling you, I couldn't tell you much about what went on up on that mountain, because I spent the whole time down on Cow Creek. But I understand that it was the soldiers that stopped it all. Just came in and told them boys to lay down their guns, and they did, too, all except for one man, one man was all, that shot at them soldiers. Well, they took care of him fast enough. Was Bad Lewis White that told me that.

"Yes, Bad Lewis, I knew him well. A regular son of a gun, he was, mean as a snake. He was a kin of mine, related through my uncle Ark. He was born over on Hell Creek, in Mingo County. He started in the mines pretty young, and he was into the union and all because he was working up on Coal River in a union mine. He was one of the ringleaders of this here miner's march. They were broken down into groups of a hundred or so, and he was leading one of them groups.

"He was the one that captured Fult Mitchell and Howard Young on that mountain. You've heard about that haven't you? Lewis's man had captured several of the deputies, Fult Mitchell, Howard Young, the speed cop, and another one, I can't remember his name, one night up in the mountain. They took them over to an old farmhouse up there, and Lewis had them tied up, planning on killing them. Now, some time before this, Lewis had been held prisoner for a while in the Logan jail by Fult Mitchell, and he wanted to give him a talking-to over that before he killed him.

"Well, as Lewis was getting ready to give him this talking-to, one of his own men come along and spit in Fult's face. This made Lewis mad, and he started cussing his man out, and getting more and more angry. 'How are you going and spitting in this man's face when I'm just about to talk to him?' he says. 'Just for that I'm not going to kill him after all.' Now, that's the facts, just as Lewis told them to me. And Fult Mitchell and Howard Young, they was let free.

"It was a few months after that when Lewis showed up in the

streets of Logan. Oh, he was a nervy son of a gun, no question about it. And he runs into Don Chafin in the street. 'Don, if you arrest me, you'll be a dead son of a bitch. One of us'll be dead, that's sure, one or t'other.' And he went on to cussing him out, like that.

"'Put down that gun,' says Don. 'I know that it was you saved Fult Mitchell's life on that mountain. And anyone that's a friend of one of my deputies is a friend of mine.' Well, Don always did like Lewis after that. 'A man with that much nerve,' he used to say, 'and you've got to like him.' Don always did like nervy ones. He was a pretty nervy fellow himself. They say he's killed a few men when he was drunk, you know.

"Now, Don and I was pretty good friends, because I worked for him getting out the votes. But we did have a falling-out a couple of times. He got word one time that I had voted for the Republican, Hatfield, and he was pretty sore, and I was out of a job.

"But, the next election come around, and when I come out of the booth, I seed a couple of his deputies there, so I held up my ballot real high so that they could see it, and I had voted a straight Democratic ticket. Well, I knew that that would get back to Don soon enough, and sure enough, it did. Within a couple of days, he called me in to see him and said, 'Little Cow'—he called me that because I was from over Cow Creek way—'Little Cow,' he says, 'I think you told me the truth before when you said that you didn't double cross me on that vote.' And I says, 'Don, would I lie to you?' And we was just like old buddies again, yes sir.

"But when things really started moving with the union around here, wasn't nothing Don could do to stop it, and he just had to go along with it. I was working over at Henlawson in 1934 when they started signing us up over there. I'm telling you, we was so happy when that happened that we had kind of celebration parade, on foot, all the way from Henlawson to Logan. A pretty long walk, too.

"Oh, we was just all mean as snakes. Ain't too many of them boys left now. I must be one of the only ones that really remembers those times. Maybe I was just lucky. Maybe I just knew how to keep friends with all sides."

JOSH CHAFIN

Cora, West Virginia

J osh Chafin satisfies one's notions about what a little old man ought to look and act like. A thoroughly delightful man, Josh twinkles, laughs toothlessly, scratches his head, rocks back and forth on his rocker, mercilessly satirizes his past enemies, and talks on and on and on. He's so deaf that he won't respond to questioning, but that's all right, because once he gets the message about what you've come for, he hardly needs any further prompting.

"There were about eight hundred ready to fight on this side, and about seven thousand on the other," says Josh of the preparations for the Blair Mountain battle. "The ones over here weren't just from Logan, but from McDowell and Mingo too.

"Well, I stuck myself in it too. I was working in the mines over to Barnabus. A deputy come by at about eleven in the night, and said, 'Anyone who doesn't come fight is fired!' Well, I didn't care about being fired, and I didn't care about fighting either, so I figured I'd go along and see what I could think up.

"Well, when I got down to the courthouse, where they was all massing up to march up there, I could see that they was all greenhorns every one of them. I wasn't so green myself, because I had just gotten back from the First World War.

"By daylight, they had all gotten into trucks and went up to the mountain. Well, I was with them.

"Well, I'm telling you, you was in more danger from another greenhorn than any miner getting to you from the other side.

"Well, we topped up at the top of the mountain. I said, 'Look, we're running into a hornet's nest we are, and let's us stick together and hang back about fifty yards.'

"Well, you know, when you make an advance, you ought to come at the enemy in rank, you know. But them asses just topped up all together in a bunch, and they come over the hill, and them union men was waiting for them on the other side and shot them down all at once. Now, we was smart, and had fallen back behind some, and we just laid down. Pretty soon, they come over the mountain, and some went this way, and some went that way, and meantimes we's just hiding out there in them bushes, me and my buddy.

"Well, I says to my buddy, 'If that's the way they're going to fight, *I'm* not going up that Blair Mountain any further!' So, we walked along the ridge until we came upon a big log. 'Right here,' I says, 'is the best place I can think of to spend the rest of *this* battle,' I says. We wasn't hid under that log two hours when they come along and tells us that John Gore was dead. Was an old preacher man killed him.[1]

"There was another incident up there, I think it was on Beech Creek. They was taking a whole battalion of state police up there to nose around. Well, there was a woman up there, and she saw them coming and she turned her light on and off, on and off, three times, which was supposed to be a signal for the miners that trouble was coming. Well, one of these deputies shot her. Just like that. Well, they started shooting at them state police and deputies right and left. And they took off, running and hollering.

"Well, the next day, they all straggled back into camp, their

1 Likely a reference to Rev. James Wilburn.

clothes hanging off them, 'Where were you?' they said to me. Well, I had just been smart, that's all.

"Well, they all regrouped, and some went out to Crooked Creek, and others up to Peach Creek holler. Well, I went out with one of them groups, but I never did fire a shot. I just sat out there on the mountain until the army come in nine days later. That day, the army sergeant come through and told us to hand over our guns and go back into Logan. But I kept mine!

"It took them forty-eight hours to get us all in.

"Yes, I was in it, but I never fired a shot. My theory, and what I told my buddy, was this: if you shoot, they'll hear you, and locate you, and they'll shoot back at you. So, the best policy is just to keep quiet about the whole thing. So that's just what I did, kept quiet."

WILLIAM GOTHARD

Cora, West Virginia

B y ten in the morning, the bench in front of the courthouse in Logan is so crowded with old men there's barely room to sit down. Every morning, the old men, all retired miners, come down to the courthouse, "loaf around," as they put it, and wait for their benefit checks to come through.

Today, "the Reverend," one of the "courthouse gang," is out on the sidewalk politicking as usual with the old men on his way to work. The Reverend has been convicted of grand vote fraud and has been sentenced to five years in the penitentiary. His case is now on appeal.

The Reverend strolls by, leans up against a parking meter, and immediately there is a cluster of old men around him, mumbling at him. He selects one for special treatment, leans over, and whispers solicitously in his ear. Bill Gothard stands up, contemptuously bites off a chaw of tobacco, chews it to a fine consistency, and spits conspicuously into the litter barrel. He glances at the Reverend out of the corner of his eye, then goes back to his place on the bench.

Bill, at eighty-seven, is one of the oldest miners in the county. He started working as a trapper in Tennessee when he was ten years old, hoboed across the mountains in a boxcar to Logan in 1908, and then worked there for over fifty more years before he retired. Bill guesses that he has spent almost seventy years as a miner. "I suspect," Bill says modestly, "that I've been through a whole lot in my lifetime. I've been over the world some."

"My way," Bill says, "was to be a neutral. I wasn't for one side or the other. I didn't bother nobody, and nobody bothered me.

"The main cheese I was working for back then, Old Boss Payne, he was as nice a coal operator as you've ever seen. He thought I was one of the best coal loaders there was in the field, I reckon. It depends on a man's work a whole lot, I guess, whether they're nice to you or not. If you're a good worker, and try to make it, they'll help you in every way they can. Now, some of these men was lazy, and loaded only one or two car of coal a day. Not me. I loaded ten or fourteen car of a day, and I'd stay as late as I had to to clean up a room, sometimes till midnight I'd stay. And Old Boss Payne, he knew it too, and he always stood behind me, when I'd have a fight with my section-boss and like that.

"My father was a union man over in Tennessee, and I was too. I always had my union card. But I'd see'd, when I got to Logan, that if I kept quiet and did my work that I wouldn't get into no trouble. Now, if I had come in here, and started talking about the union and this that and the other, they would have had me put out right quick. Well, I was satisfied with the wages I was getting. Now, Don Chafin was always good to me too. He asked me one time, he did, 'Bill, what do you think of this here union business?' 'Well,' I says to him, 'I'm a union man myself, but I don't think it's handled right, and I don't think that we need any union here in Logan County.' 'Well, I agree with you on that,' he says.

"Now this Don Chafin, he was a mixed sort, he could be real accommodating like, and then sometimes he wasn't. Now, when this Blair Mountain episode was going on, these deputies came down and tried to get me to go up there and fight. Well, I told them I wasn't raising a gun against no one, and they should go away and leave me alone. Well, they was threatening to kill me and all. But Don Chafin told them to leave me alone, that I wasn't going to cause anybody no trouble.

"And, later on, when I decided to take my family down to Virginia to work at Dante and Roda for a spell, he was real good to me, and gave me the loan of a brand-new Model T Ford to transport me down there, and told me I was welcome to come back to Logan at any time. And I did come back, too.

"Now, I was a real slick bootlegger in those days. I was always real smart, and would never sell any liquor right directly, you know. Like maybe a fellow would come along and say, you know where a body can find himself a drink of whiskey? And I'd say, sure, I don't know, but I did see a bottle lying down by the spring when I was down there this morning. It looked like water to me, but then again, it might happen to be whiskey. And sure enough, it would be whiskey, and he'd pay me three dollars for telling him where it was. Well, the judge tried to get me on it, but I just told him, I don't make whiskey, I just make cough syrup. But I'll tell you, between you and me, that cough syrup sure could cure a cough!

"I even sold to Don Chafin one time. He comes down and says to me, 'You know where a fellow can find a drink?' I says, 'No, but I'll walk over to my neighbor's and ask him if he knows. While I'm gone, you watch my shoebox for me. I wouldn't want anybody to steal it, because I've got me a brand-new pair of shoes in there.' Well, in that shoebox was a brand-new pint of whiskey. He always told me after that, whenever he seen me, that I was just the slickest bootlegger he ever seen.

"Like I was telling you, Don could be real friendly, but he had a lot of guys killed over this union business. But he was getting paid to do it, and I just figure that's human nature. Just like this here Tony Boyle,[1] now he's got his sons and daughters on the payroll, but I'd do it too if I had my hands on the kind of money he does. And Don was getting rich over it. I just figure that where there's money, men are going to get mean."

When Bill was still a child in Tennessee, a mine right near

---

1 W. A. "Tony" Boyle, president of the United Mine Workers at the time of this interview.

where he lived exploded, killing more than two hundred men.[2] The boy watched the bodies that were able to be recovered interred in a single, mass burial. Bill views his own life as being almost incidental, as if he lived always with the constant knowledge that it could happen to him too. "I'm just a coal miner, that never meant no harm to nobody," he says, and reaches for another chaw of tobacco and looks up once more to see if the Reverend has come out of the office yet for his lunch break.

---

2   This is likely a reference to the Fraterville, Tennessee, mine disaster of 1902.

CHARLES LITERAL

Logan, West Virginia

C harlie Literal is known to the old men who hang out at the courthouse in Logan as the local history buff. It is an apt description. In the trunk of his battered Chevy, which he drives to town every morning, is a five-and-dime style photograph album, embellished with gilt roses and italic writing. Inside its covers is a collection of photographs of maimed and mutilated bodies.

"This one," Charlie explains gleefully, perched on the rear end of his auto and chewing thoughtfully on his battle-scarred cigar, "is Billy Foster, that was shot up by thugs down Rum Creek. He's got two wounds, one here in the leg you notice, and a piece of his jaw is missing here. And in this next photo . . ."

And so it goes. Only God and Charlie know where he got the photos.

Every once in a while, Charlie makes a pilgrimage down past Omar to visit the grave of Devil Anse Hatfield, the family patriarch during the famed Hatfield-McCoy feud. Devil Anse is Charlie's hero. He never gets tired of telling his courthouse friends, like Bill Gothard and Jimmy Damron, about Devil Anse, and about lots of other local history, too. And he's even been known to expound on his favorite topics at one of the weekly potluck dinners at the Senior Citizens Center.

Today, Charlie is out on the bench in front of the courthouse, as usual, and he's trying to interest Jimmy Damron in his tale. He leans over and pokes at Jimmy. "Hey, Jimmy, you know about Devil Anse?" Jimmy nods. "I was related to the Hatfields, you know. My grandfathers's sister was married to Devil Anse's brother. You've heard of him?

"Devil Anse's brother was named Wall Hatfield. He was in the penitentiary over in Kentucky for being in that feud. He died some two years after they set him up in there. I was talking to his son about it last year. I said, 'Allen, where'd they bury your daddy at?' 'Somewhere out in Kentucky,' he said. 'He was dead three months before we heard about it.' Weren't no telephones in them days. And no way of getting about, either.

"Now Sid Hatfield, he was related to them too. He was the chief of police down at Matewan when they had that shoot-out down there at the depot. Yeah, I knew one of them fellows that died, and I knew some of the eyewitnesses too. The way the whole thing started, there were those Baldwin-Felts detectives, and they had been in Matewan that day. They had thrown this one lady out of her house, and her baby too. Well, them thugs had gone down to the station to go back to Bluefield for the night. And then there was a big shoot-out.

"Now, I don't know how many were killed, maybe sixteen, that was involved, and maybe six wounded, and three dead. Only one I can remember by name, and that was Mr. Felts of the detective agency, who was right there himself with them. He got shot right here, and here.[1]

"That Sid was a regular devil himself and he would have taken the credit for killing all of them thugs if he'd been given a chance to.

"Well, next thing you know, they had a warrant for Sid's arrest in McDowell County, for shooting up the coal company. He didn't

---

[1] Both the Felts brothers, Albert and Lee, were shot and killed in this incident.

do it, but they got the warrant on him anyway. Well, he and Ed Chambers, that was Sid's right-hand man, they went over there to Welch to answer the warrant. Well, it was a trap they had set for them.

"When they got there, there was a bunch of about five Baldwin-Felts men lined up there against the courthouse. Well, I knew one of the state police supposed to be bodyguarding for Sid, and he told me the whole story. Sid got to the base of the steps there, and the men said, 'Well, Sid, it's about time you got yourself in here.' And Sid started up the steps, and he turned this way, and then this way"—at this point, Charlie leaps up and gesticulates left and then right—"and *then,* just as he gets to the top of the steps, there he sees right in front of him, about fifteen foot in front of him, five Baldwin-Felts men, and *they just opened fire on him!*"

Charlie collapses back into his seat at the impact of the bullets.

"Yes, they killed both Sid and Ed that day, killed them dead. And their wives were right with them when it happened.

"Sid's wife, now I didn't think very much of her. Right before this all had come up, she was married to the mayor of Matewan. Now, he was killed in the shoot-out with the Felts detectives over at the Matewan depot. Now, I ain't *suggesting* anything, but no one knew who killed that mayor, and Sid married his wife the week afterwards. They rumored a bit that Sid had shot him along with them Felts detectives, in the middle of all the smoke and flying debris, but I wouldn't say it for a fact. And then—brother, you won't believe this!—she turned around and married one of them state police that had been there on the courthouse steps at Welch the day Sid was shot.

"Well, I don't know what ever become of her after that. I heard that that policeman left and went into the mines to work, but he didn't make much money and she was used to having plenty, you know, and they separated, and she turned around and married another fellow, and he robbed the Paintsville bank over in Kentucky to keep her happy.

"Oh, she was the prettiest little woman you've ever seen. Yes, she was. Now, I don't know what ever become of her." Bill Gothard is nodding vigorously at the thought of this latter-day Helen of Troy. The evil woman theory of history seems to be winning Charlie some listeners, and he feels encouraged to go on.

"You ever hear of this here Blair Mountain war? The northern operators supplied John L. Lewis with the money to come down here and organize. They were under organized labor up there, and the contract had run out, and having them unorganized down here was hard on them, you see. So, they told John L. to get it organized, and put all of them on an equal basis.

"Well, that's how they come, and a lot of money was spent, and a lot of men was killed. But they just couldn't do it. They'd lose orders up there, and they'd get the orders down here, and they just didn't like it.

"My favorite was Mother Jones. I remember one thing she said kind of stuck in my mind. She was talking to them automobile workers up in Detroit, and she said to them, 'Those aren't their cars, they belong to you, because you made them.' "

By this time, Charlie's cigar is all used up, and Bill's interest is waning again. He looks at the sky, figures it's a good day to go fishing, and heads off to his car. Maybe, on the way back home, he'll get a chance to stop off and pay homage at Devil Anse's grave.

PINHEAD JONES

Logan, West Virginia

P inhead Jones is the only man who regularly hangs out at the Logan Senior Citizens Hospitality Center. The ambiance of the center is something of a cross between Brother Love's Traveling Salvation Show and a ladies' bridge club. Most of Logan's old men prefer to join the boys at the courthouse and appear at the center only on Wednesday afternoons when the ladies feed them a huge potluck dinner. But Pinhead, by himself, seems quite capable of compensating for their collective absence.

Pinhead may be the most debonair gentleman in Logan. He is bald and wiry, and always comes in immaculately dressed in a jacket, brightly striped shirt, and matching fedora. He scrupulously avoids alcohol, drinks a quart of homogenized milk a day, and at eighty-five years old still rides his bicycle every day from his home to the center and back. But his favorite sport, still, is making conversation with the ladies.

Pinhead was born in Alabama in 1887. His father died when the boy was four. At age ten, Pinhead went to work in the mines. His wage of 47 cents a day—after two years, it was raised to $1.35— supported his mother and younger brother as well as himself.

Like many other Black Alabamans at the turn of the century, Pinhead soon left home and came north to the mountains looking for work in the booming extractive industries. He ended up in Shamrock, West Virginia, and worked for the Island Creek Coal Company from 1916 until 1955.

The first time he heard of the union, Pinhead remembers, was from a fellow in his mine who was from the coalfields in Pennsylvania, where the union was already strongly organized. "But when the union first come in here," he says, "the men was all afraid of it, and we had to meet out in the woods."

Sheriff Chafin offered to pay Pinhead to go up on the mountain to fight the union. He refused. "I told him I wasn't going to have nothing to do with fighting my brothers. But I was scared. I just hid out all that week."

John L. Lewis is just about the greatest man who ever lived, if you ask Pinhead. But Franklin Roosevelt ranks high on the list too. It was because of FDR, Pinhead thinks, that the miners were ever able to organize at all.

The tape recorder, for a while, seemed to almost replace the ladies as the center of Pinhead's attentions. He would hold it up real close, whisper solicitously at it, grin broadly, hold it back to judge its reaction, and then pull it to him closely again for another come-on. But it wasn't long before he was off again flirting with the real thing.

SPENCER BRINEGAR

Logan, West Virginia

Displayed on the wall of Tom Johnson's real estate office on Stratton Street is a wide-angle photograph of the Logan area, taken in 1918, probably from a nearby mountain top. The photograph is sooty and bleak, like the coal train yards, the smoke belching power plant, the imposing and jagged mountain ranges, and the almost dwarfed town which it depicts.

Tom Johnson is not an old man, and he was not living in Logan at the time the photograph was taken. He remembers, though, a man who was working in that power plant the day the photograph was taken.

Spencer Brinegar, as it turns out, worked hard for the company, and today is happily retired in an attractive apartment, completely equipped with matching furniture and piped-in music, on fashionable Dingess Street.

In 1921, at the time of the Blair Mountain "trouble," Spencer was working as a shift operating engineer at the Appalachian Power Company in Mt. Gay. When the battle started, Spencer's acquaintance, Walter Thurmond, a coal operator, came around to recruit Spencer's services. "Don't you realize," he said, "that those criminals plan to take over the whole town of Logan?" Spencer had not been duly impressed. "I've got a good job," he answered, "working ten hours a day, seven days a week to produce the electricity so you can run your coal out of this county. That's enough." The argument seemed to convince Thurmond, who went away and left Spencer alone for the duration.

One gets the impression that Spencer didn't have a very high impression of the Logan fighting forces. One day, he was on his way home from work when he noticed some commotion across the street. A young man had been issued an army rifle to take up onto the mountain to fight and hadn't known how to handle it properly. The thing had exploded while the boy was out taking his sweetheart for a walk. It had blown out a huge cavity in the sidewalk, and the shrapnel from the blast had torn the girl's silk stockings to shreds and had left her legs bleeding. Everyone all around, it seems, was quite chagrined and embarrassed.

At his job in the plant, Spencer heard rumors about every day about the goings-on on the mountain. Huntington and Logan papers carried regular reports, and Spencer got news from Dave Mitchell, the brother of Fulton and Lucian, who were later captured and then freed by Bad Lewis White and his miners on Blair Mountain. Other employees in the plant used to tell him about the men who had been killed up Crooked Creek and Mill Creek, and who had to be packed off the mountains in freight cars.

The power plant maintained a powerful steam whistle, known as "the wildcat," which Spencer was responsible for setting off to alert Logan's volunteer fire department in case of fire. During the week of fighting, a delegation visited him, and they worked out arrangements for him to set off the wildcat if the miners broke through the defensive lines on top of the mountain ridge and were on their way into the town. "But," says Spencer with obvious relief, "it never got to that point."

The reason it didn't was simple: federal troops came in and broke up the battle. Spencer knows about that, because his brother had re-enlisted in the army after the war and was among the troops sent into the area. According to his brother, the troops had split into two parties at Huntington, one going south along the Guyandotte River, through Logan, to cut off the Logan forces; the other traveling down the Coal River via St. Albans to cut off the union men. "He described it," remembers Spencer, "as a pincer effect." The effect was successful.

Spencer sums up the event this way: "I guess," he says, "that they didn't value human life very highly in those days."

ERNEST BLANKENSHIP

White's Addition, West Virginia

O ld Man Blankenship."

The other old timers knew that he remembered a lot about the old days in the coal camps. But none of them knew what the old man's first name was, or even whether he was still living.

His name is Ernest, and he *is* still living—in a single room in the basement of a home which he bought for his son with the savings from a lifetime of digging coal.

He doesn't go upstairs very often. His son, a disabled miner, and his family have their own lives to lead. The old man is proud and prefers his own room where he is sure he is not bothering anyone.

Ernest was born in 1900 in Kanawha City, West Virginia. When he was twelve, he remembers, he was "big enough to carry a bucket, and thus big enough to trap in the mines." A year later, he signed up with the other men at the mine when it was organized by the United Mine Workers. He has remained a union man ever since. "Honey," he says, "I'm a union man, and I will be as long as I live."

A year later, after his father had been shot in a brawl, Ernest moved south to McDowell County to work alongside his uncle in the mines there. Later, after a brief stint in the armed forces during World War I, he moved to Logan, and took a job under Mr. Gay at Gay Coal and Coke.

Mr. Gay—"Old Man Gay"—had a son, Harry, who was Ernest's age, and the two became close friends. "Me and him was good friends," Ernest says. "I chauffeured for him some. Wasn't but four or five cars in all of Logan at that time. We were both single then, and I used to drive him around when he'd want to go out calling on the girls. He'd go inside the house, and he'd tell me that if anyone came along, to blow that horn real hard.

"Now there was one woman, I remember, come through selling baking powders. Harry got acquainted with her. Me and him went to see her in Williamson. He said, 'Ernie, I'm going to marry that girl.' But, apparently the law was after her for something, and the state police come and got her, and we never did see her again. Now, the woman he finally did marry, she was a nurse. He met her when he was getting the treatments at Hot Springs, Maryland.

"Oh, we were the best of friends. Any job I wanted in the mines I could have. Me and him roomed together for a bit. And he even used to ask me to go stay with his mother and sister in Baltimore to take care of them when they weren't well, that's just how much he thought of me.

"One time I says, 'Harry, I'm going to leave here and find me a job somewheres else.' 'Ernie,' he says, 'how much money do you need? I'll give you anything you need.' Well, I heard him say that, and I just knew that I couldn't leave any boss that was that good to me. 'No,' I said, 'Harry, I can't leave you. You're getting too nice. I'm not going.' "

Despite their friendship, Ernest never discussed unionism with Harry, although, throughout this period, he remained a card-carrying member of the UMWA. "Lord," he says, "if I'd ever mention it, it would have been the end of me. No one, no one, knew that I belonged."

Ernest wasn't kidding when he said that it was dangerous

to talk union. One day, he remembered, he got to talking with another miner in his boarding house about the union, and a company spy overheard the conversation. "Well, the next day, I was down in the basement of the courthouse over at Logan. And I run into this spy, and he was with one of the deputies. He called me a redneck. 'This is one of them rednecks,' he says to his buddy. I told him to his face that he was nothing but a son of a bitch. Well, he pulled his gun, aimed to shoot me. Lukey Curry, the deputy, grabbed that fellow to keep him from shooting me. Well, I figure I was just lucky that time.

"It was just about that bad. Now, there may have been a lot of other union men at that mine where I worked, but I never did find any. Some may have been union members, like me, but they kept it a secret, and I never knew it because none of them ever dared to talk about it to anyone else.

"We didn't have no successes at all until 1933. I was working up at Monniker at the time. We had a real bad time getting it started. We tried to meet out on the tracks, and the detective run us off. We had to just slip around. We finally got a place in Logan to meet, in the basement of the building where the bus depot is now. A few of us could go at a time, and get signed up, and then come back to Monniker, and convince some more, until finally we had a majority. Finally, then, the company recognized us.

"Well, it just about heaven when we finally got the union. A lot of things went to changing right away. For one thing, when I first went in the mines, I had to work in water, in cold water, right here it would come up to your thighs. Well, you'd get sweaty from all that heavy work, and hot, and your feet would be in that cold water. I got sick from it many a time. But when the union come in, they had to get rid of that water.

"And another thing. Logan Hospital used to be a butcher shop, not a hospital. I was in there one time with a broken arm from the mines. There was fellows in there with everything in the book, broken backs, everything. Well, you should have seen those bedbugs and roaches. It was so bad that them bedbugs would get down in those men's casts, and they would go crazy with pain, and they'd get them these wires and stick down in the casts trying to pick them bedbugs out. Oh, it was hell. But when the union come in, you talk about cleaning up a hospital!

"The union did a lot of other things, too. Used to be, you had to do all your shopping at the company store. Was no choice in the matter. Peddlers would try to come around, you know, and they'd chain off the road leading to the camp so that they couldn't come in. Really, that is facts. Now, we got that changed, so that you could shop anywhere you chose, and that helped to keep the prices of food down. And you got paid for your dead-work, and they couldn't dock your cars for the slate in them anymore.

"And if we had a grievance, we could take it to the mine committee, and they'd take it up with the bosses and iron it out. If things didn't get settled then, we'd strike. We had several strikes over this, that, and the other. Before the union, well, there weren't any strikes at all then. No, sir. We didn't hardly even know what a strike was, then.

"Yes, things certainly got to changing.

"Honey, I really know what the union is. All of us old fellows do, the ones that fought for it. I'm seventy-two years old. It's been a long life. I'm not well. I was in the hospital last year, had one collapsed lung and about everything else wrong with me you could think of. The doctor told my son that there was no way I could live through it. But I did. I guess I just had some things that kept me going. Like the memory of my wife, she was a wonderful, wonderful woman. And that letter that Harry Gay wrote saying that I was one of the finest employees that had ever worked for him. And my son and his family, fine family. But maybe of all the things that really keep me going on, the union's the one."

VIRGIE BROWNING

Verdunville, West Virginia

W hen L. Dow Browning retired in 1964, he had worked as a miner for the Gay Coal and Coke Company for sixty years. The company invented a special award for the occasion. In the history of Logan County mining, it was an employment record of almost unheard-of longevity. Threatened by slate falls and deadly air on one hand, and automation on the other, few of the miners in southern West Virginia have been able to work even the twenty consecutive years necessary for a UMWA pension. "Yes," his wife Virgie says, "I do believe he broke some sort of record."

Today, Dow is nearly totally deaf and suffers from dementia. His wife, however, who is younger than he, still remembers life in the Gay coal camp in the nonunion era.

The couple were not yet married at the time of the Blair Mountain battle, but Virgie remembers that "Old Man" Gay, the owner of the Gay Company, had been against the union, and had recruited his men to fight against it. "Dow told me," she remembers, "that they put him to work clearing the ballpark. They brought planes in here, you know, to bomb the miners on Blair Mountain, and they took over the ballpark to use as a landing field."

Virgie had a great deal to say about Old Man Gay and his

son, Harry, who took over the business in the late twenties. "He was real good to all his working men," she says of the Old Man. "When he was planning to retire, he made special arrangements for Dow so that he wouldn't be fired, ever. He took care of his men like that, you know.

"His son, Harry, was just like him too, real friendly and nice. He used to go inside the mines every day, and he knew all the men, each and every one of them. Before he was married, Harry boarded in the house where all the scrip writers and office men lived. I used to wash and clean there, and I knew him well. He took his meals with a woman across the street from up in the camp, and after dinner, lots of times he would come over and sit on the porch and talk.

"There was a little schoolhouse down here at the mouth of Mud Fork, but they used it as a church house. Well, all the miners would go to Sunday school every week, and Harry would come there too. Nowadays, you know, you'd never see a coal operator in the same church with his miners; he'd go to a higher one. But not Harry. When he'd pass the people that lived in the camp, he'd yell and say, 'Don't forget Sunday school in the morning!'

"Every Christmas they'd have a party at that same schoolhouse for the children. Harry would buy gifts for all of them, and they'd have a tree, and give out fruit and things like that.

"Another time, I remember," she says, "a man was killed up here in the mines, a fellow named McDonald. In those days, the miners couldn't afford any decent burial, and we didn't have any burial fund dues. Well, Harry rented a funeral home for him, and he paid for the whole thing, just like he was his own kin.

"Yes, he was a good man. Of course, the wages weren't nothing, and he wouldn't stand for any union talk, but the men wouldn't say anything against him hardly. His men, they liked him, and he liked them, and I think he more or less took them under as a family."

GEORGIE MCCLOUD

Harts, West Virginia

Georgie McCloud had prepared in advance a written statement which discussed her family history and the coming of
the union to the southern coalfields. "I just decided to write
it down," she says, "because it just all come into my head after
you called me." The bulk of the interview consisted of Georgie's
reading the statement aloud, explaining and elaborating as she
went along.

Georgie grew up in the 1910s in a hollow in the northwestern
part of Logan County. Her extended family was close knit, and
she was able to remember in detail—an indication, no doubt, of
the importance of the information to her—the convolutions of
her family tree. Today, she lives in a farmhouse in a very isolated
area in the mountains. She expressed in many ways during the
interview, in gesture, in silence, in choice of incidents and the
words in which she expressed them, that she felt deeply grieved
that the family had, since her childhood, split apart, and part of the
family had moved away to the towns and away from those of their
relatives, like Georgie, who had chosen to remain up the hollows.

When Georgie was still a young girl, her two older brothers,
Wayne and Gordon, like most men of the county in that day, were
forced to take sides on the union question. Wayne, a coal miner,

supported the union cause. Gordon, however, had taken a job under Don Chafin, and served for a time as part of his personal bodyguard. Georgie remembers with special clarity one incident, in which union men attacked Chafin at the courthouse and were beaten back by Gordon and others in his bodyguard. Georgie suspects that Wayne was among the attackers. The incident, a bewildering one, no doubt, to a young girl brought up to believe in complete loyalty to her family, was told haltingly, punctuated by long periods of silence.

Finally, she seemed to have found a phrase that summed up how she felt about the experience. "Yes," she said, "that's it. It was just one brother on one side, and the other brother on the other."

Georgie had heard about the Battle of Blair Mountain, but hidden away in the hollow, she hadn't witnessed it herself. She remembered many small details about the event that she had been told: that the sheriff's men had been supplied with khaki uniforms, that Mother Jones had visited the miners in Logan County and had addressed them from the rail depot at Mt. Gay, and that many men had been killed up on the mountain. But she did remember firsthand what she—and presumably other members of her family who were at home—had felt at the time: "You could almost hear a pin drop. That was right! Everyone was scared!"

Georgie seemed very pleased by the visit and lavished home-grown vegetables on her guest, along with a tour of the chicken coop and a lengthy discourse on the fine points of breeding rabbits. Before her interviewer left, she stressed the point, just to make sure: "I want you to know this," she said, "that everything that I've told, they're the *real facts*."

IRA HAGER

Meadowbrook Hills, West Virginia

ra Hager was born in 1883 on a farm in Lincoln County, West Virginia. His father, at one time a prosperous farmer, was blinded in combat in the Civil War and was forced to turn over the management of his property to his eldest son, Ira's brother. The farm failed during the agricultural depression of the 1890s, "the Cleveland Panic," as Ira calls it. Ira recalls a childhood of struggling to find enough to eat and pay taxes so that the farm would not be foreclosed.

Very early, Ira wanted to learn to read. With no money for books, his enterprising mother traded a rooster for a secondhand reader. "I learned to read," Ira remembers, "by reading the story about the fox and the duck. The fox, he wanted to get himself a duck, but they were all out in the river where he couldn't get to them. Well, he found himself a log, and floated downstream, and circled around a bit, and stretched himself out on the log some— and caught himself two ducks! Well, that interested me. I figured that if I could read that, I could read anything."

The story's motif of ingenious self-help seemed to forecast Ira's own development. At sixteen, he left home to make some money, lived in "camp cars," and worked on the railroad. The boss under whom he worked soon recognized the boy's ability and put him to work "keeping the books." Finally, Ira saved enough money to hire himself a private teacher. He then went on to Marshall College, and from there, to law school.

In 1914, Ira Hager, then thirty-one years old, came to Logan, West Virginia, and set up practice as one of the town's first professionals. Logan, in those days, was, Ira recalls, "a pretty, clean little town." Most of the inhabitants were, like Ira, professionals— merchants, bankers, doctors, lawyers. However, most of them, unlike him, were associated in some way with the coal industry. Outside the town proper, though, things were different. There, Ira remembers, "it was just one coal camp after another." Ira learned quickly of the conditions under which the miners were forced to work and live, and of the system of "retainers" maintained by the coal industry to keep the union from organizing. "It was a bloody system in Logan County. I saw those miners being mistreated." Ira was later to devote much of his career to helping their cause.

In 1921, Ira received a call from a relative in Mingo County, who told him that an armed march on the county was imminent. Ira knew that he would most likely be called on to fight against the union. He also suspected that one of his brothers, a union miner, would be involved in the invasion. He packed up immediately and left the county and stayed with his family in Lincoln County for the duration of the Blair Mountain affair.

The twenties were violent years in Logan County. Soon after the labor trouble on the mountain was over, Ira's brother, the miner, was killed in a shoot-out in Boone County, to the north. Ira went up to handle the prosecution. But the defendant, a bootlegger, had the good fortune to be tried by a jury of men who worked the same bootlegging ring, and Ira was unable to get a conviction.

In his many years of legal practice, Ira remembers handling no less than fifty murder cases. "There were so many," he says, "that I can't even remember the details."

In 1924, Ira was one of the leading figures in a Republican coalition organized to break the strength of the coal industry–dominated Democratic regime in the county. Ira was terrorized.

His office was broken into and his files scattered on the floor. The Republicans were not allowed to speak in the schools or other places normally used by political candidates, so they were forced to take their case out into the fields. But they always drew crowds. They sought to appeal to the miners and their families. "But the miners," Ira says, "couldn't seem to stick together, even though they knew what the Democrats had done to them. Why, I've seen a man be beat up by mine thugs, and then turn right around and vote Democratic." The miners, he felt, had been so badly intimidated that they were unable to present a solid front on election day. The Republicans had some success that year but slipped back again in the next election.

During the thirties, Ira prepared several affidavits detailing the violation of the miners' civil rights by the company-paid deputy sheriffs. This work was later praised, he says, by John L. Lewis as having "paved the way for the union in Logan County." He declines to discuss these affidavits now, however. The violations, he says, were "too bad even to think about now."

Ira hopes, if he lives long enough, to write a book—about the early settlers or Logan County, about the timber industry, about the Spanish-American War, in short, "about the things that happened in my day."

HARRY DINGESS

Barnabus, West Virginia

Harry Dingess was born in Logan County in 1911. His father had grown up on a farm and had held all manner of jobs to support his growing family, from saw logging to team driving to bossing prisoners on a chain gang. Finally, when Harry was a little boy, his father took a job as a deputy sheriff under Don Chafin.

"We had always been good Democrats, and we had a large family and could bring in a lot of votes. I'd say that that had more to do with it than anything else, probably," Harry recalls. "And then again, you had to be pretty nervy in them days to be a deputy sheriff. Why, I've seen my father walk a prisoner into jail from the head of Mud Fork, some seven or eight miles. But then, he was good at that; he'd had a lot of experience bossing the chain gang. Most of his work, though, was just routine police work, breaking up drunken brawls over a woman in the camps, and things like that. Wasn't too much of it connected with labor trouble."

Harry was ten years old when "the trouble on Blair Mountain" broke out. He was shuttled off to a relative's home, while his father worked running supplies up and down the mountain to Chafin's forces. As Harry was told at the time, wages were good, and the miners didn't want the union anyways. They were just out fighting to protect the miners from those violent "rednecks" from up north.

At age eleven, Harry went to work saw logging, and has been working ever since. ("Quite a work experience, don't you think?") He lived in a logging shanty. When it was time for the camp to move, the families would tie ropes around the houses, put the privy on top of the house, hook the whole rig up to a mule team, and move on to the next site. During the Depression, the business failed, and Harry went into the mines. He has worked for the coal industry, on and off, ever since. Today, he bosses on a strip-mining operation in Mingo County. He was interviewed at the mine site.

Harry had always been very close friends with Don Chafin. Towards the end of Don's life, they shared a hunting cabin in Ohio. Don was, he recalls, "one of the best persons I ever knew. You could swear by him. When he told you something, well, that was exactly the way it was." Don was a real politician, always doing favors for people. "Labor didn't have a better friend than Don in Logan County," he says. "I've seen him give many a ten-dollar bill to a miner who'd told him a hard-luck story."

From 1946 to 1949, Harry served as deputy sheriff, and from 1949 to 1960 as constable. He is now running for sheriff. "When I was a little boy," he says, "I wanted to be two things when I grew up. A team driver and sheriff. Well, I've done made the first part a long time ago. Now, I'm aiming for the second."

WILLIE EPPS

Fireco, West Virginia

Willie Epps lives in the Black section of Fireco, across the tracks from most of his fellow retired miners. He began mining in the days when "you got two and a half for a ten-hour day." Before the Depression, he worked up to the position of coal loader, earning take-home pay of five dollars a day. The Depression and the establishment of the United Mine Workers coincided; Roosevelt signed "the legal organizing law" in 1933, Willie recalls. During the worst of the Depression years, he was working "two, three days a week, maybe two, three dollars, all scrip." The benefits of the union were not realized until the war years, he said.

Despite the hard years, he worked nineteen years in the Ray-core mines and then thirteen in the Lillybrook mine. Both were unionized, and he had no difficulty getting his pension. With this money and his savings, he bought a house in Lillybrook's camp, Fireco.

"I wasn't a man for running around, I worked. To tell you the truth, I loved it. When I got cut off—I got cut off for five years when they shut it down—I used to come out on the porch and give a little cry, hearing the old shifts, and wanting to go back to work. I was making good money, had a good boss, a good mine, a good, clean mine. I tell you now, if the mines was still the way they was . . ." The introduction of machinery led to shutdowns at the Lillybrook mine. "The coal was top-chute, the machines, they went too quick, wouldn't let the roof settle, so down it came." The Lillybrook shaft is presently abandoned.

Willie was a committeeman for thirteen years and is a Miller supporter.[1] The worst thing he sees happening is the division between young and old miners. "They lay off the old miner, got seniority . . . [and] hire on a young fellow, don't know anything about the mines. Me, they got to pay twenty-five a shift, I know my rights, but the young men, they can give him ten. He don't know."

The machines also called for a different kind of miner than those Willie worked with during his active years. Skill in mining became less important than machine knowledge. And the machines meant fewer miners. "There's ten where there used to be forty." He believes that the smaller number of miners has reduced the total number of fatalities, although the percentage of workers injured and killed is higher.

He finds the dust levels no worse now than they used to be. "Used to be, if you got the black lung, you'd call it anything, but we didn't know it was this black lung." He filed for and received his black lung compensation.

Willie Epps doesn't worry about much. His house is paid for; his yard is full of chickens. All his sons have moved away and gotten jobs in the city. The pictures of their families cover the front room walls. "They all educated, talk high! Lord, they come in and talk, I just nod my head, they talking so high." He worries about the old miners who still don't have their compensation. He's glad that young Black people are getting good jobs outside of Raleigh County, although he misses their presence.

---

1 The term "committeeman" refers to a member of the union grievance committee. "Miller" is Arnold Miller, the Miners for Democracy candidate for the presidency of the United Mine Workers of America. Miller was elected in December 1972, defeating incumbent W. A. "Tony" Boyle.

Willie remembers the stories of early organizing in Raleigh County and has told them to many of the VISTA volunteers that come in to interview him. He missed most of the excitement, since he didn't arrive in Raleigh County until 1930, after leaving a job in Virginia. One of his favorite stories is about Mother Jones holding a rally in a nearby hollow. He talks as though he were there, but it happened ten years before he arrived in Raleigh County. He's a good storyteller, and he tells the story of Mother Jones complete with stories of guns and hundreds of miners gathering at night to hear her.

Willie believes "the miners was equal in the mines," even though most of the supervisory positions were denied to Black people. According to him, this was a reverse blessing: "I know all kinds of white folks, my age, haven't got their pension. Us colored people, we put in our time and got our money, but the company would carry the white folks, make them little bosses. The UMWA doesn't pay pensions for any bosses, so they never got any."

Now, he says, it's hard for Black people to get jobs in the mines. "You go up to a mine, you see a hundred white faces, you won't see any Black faces, maybe one, but not many." This is partly because young Blacks don't want to work in the mines, he said, and partly because "the companies don't want them, they wouldn't give my boys nothing to do." This bothers Willie, but he can't see any way it's going to change.

LUTHER KEEN

Holden, West Virginia

T hey was just ripe for picking," Luther Keen says of the Logan County coal miners to whom he administered the union obligation in 1933. He smiles broadly. "And I thank the dear Lord that I was able to help Him pick!"

Luther, now seventy-one years old, began working at the Island Creek mines in 1917 as a brakeman, and worked there until his retirement in 1958.

When the union forces marched south to Blair in 1921, Luther remembers, miners were recruited by the hundreds by their foremen, supplied with money, food, clothing, and high-powered rifles, and taken up on the mountain to defend the county. Fortunately, Luther says, he had been injured in a slate fall several weeks before, and was in the hospital at the time, and thus managed to avoid participating. "But I wouldn't have gone even if I hadn't been in the hospital," Luther points out emphatically. "It probably would have cost me my job, though. It's not that I was afraid, no sir, but I believed in the union, and I had a brother-in-law was a union miner on the other side."

Even though he wasn't there, Luther had heard a lot about it. "Yes, that was a real war, sister. If they hadn't sent the army in here, they would have had a real slaughter on their hands."

All through the twenties, those years when, as Luther puts it, "they had the union pretty well run out of the state, there were still plenty of men that was union men at heart. But they dreaded these overlords that was protecting the companies. Don Chafin had this county one hundred percent under control. You may have been for the union, but brother, you'd better not mention it, because they were tough on anyone was known to be leaning towards the union. They didn't care nothing for a man's life. You know the old expression—'If you kill a man, you just hire another, but if you kill a mule, you have to buy one'—They cared more for a mule than they did for a man, in those days."

In 1933, Luther actively assisted the district officers in their organizing drive in the Logan field, and he later became president of the first local union, No. 5813, at the Holden No. 7 mine. "Once we had the Blue Eagle behind us," he says, "things began to happen real fast.[1] These men had been living like slaves in these coalfields all their lives. This was during the worst of the Depression, and they was ragged, hungry, even barefooted, yes they was, that was their condition, honey. It was beyond your imagination. We'd get up and address crowds of them—like that time at the Ellis ballpark, when maybe fifteen or twenty thousand of them turned out. They knew that they didn't have anything to lose, and any gain would be better than what they had. We went to the people, and the people came to us, that was all there was to it. It was real easy to get ninety-five percent of the men at each mine to sign up with us.

"Of course, there was some that didn't come in right away, but that was because they was afraid that they'd lose their jobs. In those cases, we'd just get together a few hundred men and go march on the mine that wasn't coming in with us, and we'd give they a little pep talk and *bring* them in. Once they got the fear of the devil out of them, and they saw that this thing was for real— and believe me, *it was*—they'd come right in behind us. The worst

---

1 The "Blue Eagle" refers to the National Recovery Administration, established in 1933 by the National Industrial Recovery Act. Its symbol was a blue eagle.

place we had to organize were the Youngstown captive mines at Dehue, over on Rum Creek. The operators was there with their high-powered machine guns and everything. But this time, we had the protection of the law, and they came around eventually.

"When we finally succeeded, after all these years, in getting the union organized in there, we thought that we were going to get the world with a little red fence around it, just about. But it wasn't that easy. First thing, the Progressives come in here—they was a dual union from over in Illinois—and tried to bust us up.[2] A few took up with them. There are a few, you know, in any crowd, that will go along with anything. But we run them out of here pretty fast.

"And we had quite a lot of trouble with wildcat strikes. There hadn't been any strikes at all, you know, all those years when the men had been working nonunion, and all of a sudden, when the union come in here, they had a lot of things on their minds, and they kept shutting down the mines, even when the district officials didn't want it. I always stood with the union officials on these things. That's one reason, I think, that the company reinstated me in my job. They had fired me, you know, in 1933, when they saw what a dynamite organizer I was."

Luther was asked what he thought would have happened if the New Deal legislation had not been passed, and things had gone on as they had. "Lord only knows," he exclaimed. "We'd probably still be living under slavery today."

---

2 The Progressive Miners of America, later known as the Progressive Mine Workers of America, was a rival union based in Illinois that formed in a split from the UMWA in 1932.

EDWARD PERRY

Holden, West Virginia

T he two-lane asphalt road up the mountain to Ed Perry's house is almost impassable for ordinary passenger cars. It hasn't been repaired since 1960. That year, the small No. 22 Holden mine to which the road leads exploded, burning eighteen men alive. Some will tell you that gas and dust levels in the mine at the time were way above the legal maximum. Island Creek Coal Company permanently shut down the operation and, of course, stopped repairing its access road.

There aren't many houses around Ed's now. After the mine closed, the company offered to sell the company-owned houses to the families that lived in them. They didn't have much reason to stay. For the few families that still included an able-bodied man, there was no work, and for the rest, the small camp held bad memories. The company found only four buyers, all old men who had spent their whole working lives in and around the No. 22 mine. The company brought in a wrecker, and destroyed all but these four homes, one of them Ed Perry's.

Today, Ed spends most of his time sitting in a metal chair on the lawn outside his home looking at the mountains. Sometimes, one of the "good old boys" who have known Ed for years will come by to talk. Sometimes, he works for a while "picking around" in his vegetable garden, and his wife will come out to help. "She'll just *know*, and, first thing you know, I'll look up and there she'll be, working alongside of me.

"I've always held my head up as high as I could get it," Ed says quietly. "Always, ever since I started in the mines in 1918—that was a long time ago, you know!—my sentiment was always one hundred percent behind organized labor. That's a thing just as natural as breathing. Your sentiments and your feelings are to better yourself. When they was trying to organize, the miners were seeking equality. They were seeking to better themselves and their children."

Ed stretches his hands forward in the air, feeling for words with which to translate his experience into terms his interviewer will understand. "Well, it was sort of like this here women's lib business." He laughs suddenly at the boldness of his analogy. "Now just think, yourself," he says, pointing to his interviewer, "just suppose that you was cast down to the lot of a scrubwoman. Now, you'd want to better yourself, wouldn't you? That's in God's law as well as man's. Well, that's what we miners was doing, seeking a betterment.

"They didn't have any union where I started work over at Cora, in Logan County, in 1918. But, they came out on strike in Mingo County. They was trying to organize, you know. The coal operators was naturally against organized labor. Those miners had it pretty rough. Now, I don't know this for myself, because I was in Logan, but I've heard tell, and I know it for a fact, that the company got eviction warrants and they got a bunch of detectives from over in Virginia, these Baldwin-Felts agents, to come and set them out of their houses. And these men and their families had to set up in tents. It stayed that way for many months.

"Now, I'll say this, in anything that's worthwhile, there is always a little friction to start it off. It don't start smooth on both sides. And right here, I'd say, both sides did a little bit of the dirty work. Now, I wasn't implicated in no violence like some of these fellows was, I didn't believe in that. It was just fist and skull, and rock throwing, mostly. One little incident I remember. They was bringing in some men from Kentucky or somewhere, I don't remember. They was scabs, union busters. Well, when they come in there on the transportation, those boys were waiting for them at the station, and if they didn't ever take off after them, running down the street and throwing rocks at them and trying to kill them. They got out of there that night. That particular time, it didn't build up to no bloodshed.

"Now, another time, one of these Baldwin-Felts agents—they was just common strikebreakers, you know—those operators used them kind of like a whip to break them up—set a woman out of her house on a cot, right in the cold. Well, this was how the trouble started. The miners was wanting it to start no doubt. It wound up that they all got shot. Two miners got killed in it, and the Baldwin-Felts agents, and the mayor of the town of Matewan. And Sid Hatfield, the leader of the miners that day, it wasn't long before they shot him too, over at Welch.

"Well, there was a big reaction to that. There was no transportation in those days, or otherwise they would have all crowded in there by the hundreds. None of us liked that because he was a friend to organized labor. But there was no aftermath to it. The law in Mingo County, just the way it was all over the mining districts, was controlled by the coal operators. Don Chafin over in Logan, too, now he got ten cents a ton on all coal mined, and he just about was the law in that county.

"Well, it just went on like this for a long time, and it was getting worse and worse, and harder and harder to live. In 1931, I was working at a real small mine here in Logan County. I liked the job, even though the wages were nothing. The fellow that owned the job was real sociable and nice, and he used to come down and talk to us a lot. But that mine went bankrupt, and even today it's still sitting there, just the same as it was when it closed back then. People was starving during that depression. Wages got down to 45 cents a car for a four-ton car, or that's what I hear, in some places.

"Well, we was all union men at heart, ninety-five percent of us was, and we was doing everything possible to get the union in here, but we were more or less on our own, you know, we was just working men with no capital. Help had to come from outside. Sentiment was running that way, but the union still didn't go too good until we got the sentiment of the people in power. The union was the only thing they had. But the operators was never going to break down and bring them up, you know.

"Well, about the way I see it, as long as you're down and out, and everybody's walking on you, you aren't going to get much sentiment. But, once you got a toehold, public sentiment will begin edging in your favor. As soon as you get to fighting back, pretty soon you've got someone there pushing for you. Now, Roosevelt was a rich man, but he was a humanitarian too, and he could see both sides of the picture. All we needed then to square everything off and to remove the violence was to be granted the right to collective bargaining. Well, Roosevelt did that for us in 1933. Then they was started up the ladder, and they come up pretty good.

"The miner, he had always been kind of like a slave in everyone's opinion, even his own. Well, that all come about to breed a sentiment in their hearts to come up, not to accept it laying down, but to come up to a place in society where they was acceptable, by their striving. And they've got it, too. It was by the older miners' having these sentiments of equality, that's why working miners today are accepted in any society."

BEA CURTIS

Williamson, West Virginia

Bea Curtis lives in public housing in Williamson. She is on welfare and active in the county's welfare rights movement. Her health is poor, and at times, she's spent months in the hospital. She is active despite the threats of the local welfare office to withdraw her hospital card, which would mean death, since she only "draws" eighty-some dollars a month.

Bea's parents moved to the southern coalfields in 1921 from the tin mines of Alabama. Several trainloads of Black miners and former field hands were brought to the southern fields at the same time, when the fields were being developed with nonunion labor. Her father had several jobs in the mines. Once, while working at Matewan, their entire coal camp became involved in a wildcat strike. The company dispossessed the entire camp, in the middle of winter. "We had to get the tents. I wasn't real big then, about seven or eight, but I had to help with the cooking. It was deathly cold, and the tents would keep catching on fire from a coal stove got too close to the tent." They spent the winter there while her father looked for other work. He finally found a mine above Williamson that would hire him.

He stayed with the company and became a union member during the organizing drive in the early 1930s. She remembers him as a hardworking miner. Later, during the mechanization drive of the fifties, he was laid off and died several years later.

Bea tells a story of guerilla-like activity carried on by the Black miners to assist the miners of Wise County, Virginia. "These men would go from here at night. They'd sneak off in cars, no one knowing where they'd gone. Mothers, you know, couldn't tell the children. They'd sneak off with guns. They were horrible times." Evidently, even though the laws passed during the New Deal gave workers the right to organize, the operators in Wise were determined to resist unionization. So, miners from different counties including Mingo became "roving pickets," backing up the picket line with guns.

Bea's husband was a miner for a while, and he also worked around town. He died in an industrial accident. There was no compensation, so she had to go on welfare, particularly after her health went bad.

From Bea's house, the sound of the Norfolk and Western coal cars can be heard day and night. When she goes shopping, she has to ride under the tracks of the N & W yard. She can't afford the taxi ride downtown very often, but her legs won't let her walk. Sometimes friends can spare enough time to come by and take her out, but often they don't.

The sign at the bridge across the Tug River to Williamson reads: "Welcome to the billion-dollar coalfields."

OTIS KINSER

Logan, West Virginia

I have learned," Otis Kinser says slowly, "not to do anything, and to keep my mouth shut. There were always lots of things that I wanted to say. Sometimes, I'd go and say them secretly, behind their backs, you know. But most of the time, I was afraid to say them at all. I'd just keep it to myself. I was never served by a warrant in my life. I've never seen the inside of a jail. Now, I ain't bragging on myself, and I ain't patting myself on the back, because I'm telling you this. But I wanted to live. And I did. I'm seventy-two years old now.

"Before the union came into this field, we didn't have any protection of any kind. The law didn't protect you—they was for the thugs. The deputy sheriffs, that is, but we called them thugs. I've seen them do things that was awful, many a time. I'd seen them one day, in a gang, and they'd been drinking, and they'd be riding down the street of our camp, and maybe one of them would say something funny, and he'd throw his hat into the air, and maybe three or four bullets would be shot through it before it come down. Sure, I'd seen this, several times. And it's awful, too, to see someone you know pistol-whipped—I bet you've never seen that—hit across the head with a blackjack, or a pistol, for no reason.

"The union, when it was trying to come in here, it was trying

121

to help the men, I know it was. But the people here, they'd get scared you see, would get afraid. As near as I can figure, there was people paid to spread stories about them. They called the union men 'rednecks' and said that they was outlaws, and that they was going to get them, you know. People thought that they wasn't even human. And when someone would tell them the union was coming, they'd just get out of the way. Was no way they could get these men to stick together."

LEE JOHNSON

Monaville, West Virginia

L ee Johnson put particularly succinctly what many of the miners who, like him, were working in Logan County at the time of the armed march, said: "Those of us that didn't know what organized labor was went up there on Blair Mountain to fight against the invaders. But those of us that did wouldn't have any part of it."

Lee grew up in Milton, West Virginia, where his father worked driving a team at an oil and gas well. At age sixteen, a friend told Lee that he could find him a job in a newly opened mine in Logan County. Lee left home and began working at the nonunion mines at Ethel, up the Dingess Run to the north of the town of Logan. It was the beginning of a lifelong career in mining.

"I never even heard of the union," he says, "until those men started coming over Blair Mountain to organize this side. They did their best to see that we didn't know anything about it. Don Chafin was about like the president of the United States in this county at that time, and he was, you know, given ten cents a ton on the coal taken out of here to keep the union out. They fought the union about as hard as they could. The bosses, if you did something they didn't like, well, you just didn't have a job, that's all."

"Well, I understand that they were on that mountain because

they had come to organize the mines here in Logan County. I could hear the rifle and machine gun fire from off the mountain and all, but I wouldn't go up there, even though Chafin was bossing us to go up there just like we was soldiers, or something. I didn't feel it was my place to be up there, so I went and stayed with relatives in Chapmanville. Well, they kept them from organizing this field at that time."

From that time on, Lee felt more advanced than many of his fellow miners in his understanding of trade unionism. Despite the efforts of the operators and their deputies, some men were able to join the union secretly. Several years after the armed march—Lee thinks it was in 1925—he and several others at the Holden No. 7 and No. 8 mine clandestinely took the union obligation, well off in the woods behind the camp.

"In one sense of the word, we were all union men," he says. "But we had to keep it strictly secret, because there was no chance that the operators would recognize us at that point, not without some backing. It was just like building up anything else, you know. Until we got strong enough, we had to keep it to ourselves. Maybe a dozen or so would join the union at one place, maybe a few more at the next place. By the time Roosevelt gave us the right to organize, in 1933, well, all we needed was the go-ahead, and we were ready to start rolling."

The key period in the growth of union sympathy among the miners, Lee feels, was the Depression. "Talk about hard times," he scoffs. "*Then*, you were lucky to work two days a week. When you ate a meal, you were never sure when you were going to have the chance again. And if you didn't have a job, there was no use looking for one. And, if you did have one, you wasn't making nothing, only enough to live off of, you know." It was, he says, after 1928 that the men began to believe that the union was the only thing that could help them, "that if it wasn't for the United Mine Workers of America, we'd all be hurting."

When the union was finally organized in Logan in 1933, the men were ready. Thousands turned out for the first organizing meeting in the ballpark. It was, Lee thinks, the biggest gathering he has ever attended.

"If I knew then what I know now," Lee reflects, "and if I had my life to live over, coal mining would be the last job I'd look for." But he realizes that he never really had that option. "All of the boys my age, I guess, ended up in the mines."

"WEBSTER SMITH"

Holden, West Virginia

W ebster Smith" asked that his name not be used, so this is a fictional one.

"I began working in the mines in Logan County when I was eighteen years old. I remember really well the night that Don Chafin got us mobilized to go and fight the miners that were invading from up north. A deputy came around and roused up the foreman. It was about two o'clock in the morning. He was enlisting men to 'stop the rednecks,' as he said.

"He said that we'd get double time for our efforts plus good treatment later on. Well, I didn't think that much of the company or the job for that matter. I didn't have much stake in my job, so I just didn't go. But the men with the really key jobs, I figure they just naturally catered to the wishes of their employer. They had to.

"But I didn't stay in the mines long. I left, and went back to school, got a degree in accounting, and came back and worked for many years for Island Creek as a scrip writer and bookkeeper.

"Things got pretty rough around here when they were organizing the union. Things got really split into two camps. If a miner wasn't going along with the rest of them, they'd tie him up with a rope and drag him up some lonely hollow until, by God, he came around. And Chafin and his gang were fighting it right to the end, too. And we payroll men were right in the middle, you know, we supported them organizing, but we didn't come into the organization, you know.

"Well, I've worked hard all my life, and my wife and I have this house, and we're proud of it, especially our garden. I feel I've earned this."

SID CONLEY

Mud Fork, West Virginia

S id Conley, now seventy years old, worked for the Island
Creek Coal Company from 1918 until his retirement several years ago.

Sid can remember the miners talking about the union as early
as 1919. He had a close friend named Clifford who worked with
him as a trackman at Island Creek. Clifford had formerly worked
in union mines in the anthracite fields in Pennsylvania. Clifford
talked with Sid about how much better it was under union conditions, and he shared with him some of the union literature he
had brought south with him. Sid knew from this time on that he
wanted to be a union man.

As so many have added, however, the men weren't able to
organize. The reason, to Sid, was simple: "It was due to the enforcement of the sheriffs and their deputies, and the militia too. The
powers just didn't want it, and we had no protection. If you talked
union, you were just fired, or blackballed, that's all."

John L. Lewis sent organizers into Logan County. Their first
assignment was to go house to house and assess the degree of
union sympathy among the working miners. Sid was among those
they interviewed. He describes the contact this way: "He asked

us what we thought would be the best thing for the people to do, and what we thought about the union, and did we think organized labor would be of help to the people here. He was asking for suggestions, you know. Well, I just answered him blank and bold: 'Yes,' I said. 'I'm doing too much time for the amount I'm making, and I believe that the union would help.' "

Within a month, ninety percent of the miners, Sid thinks it was, had taken the obligation. But that wasn't to say, he adds, that all the men were "educated to trade unionism." "It was more like a bright idee that they had," he says, "that they had gotten from the men would have been up north, like my friend Clifford. Most of their information was from verbal sources." It wasn't until the union officials came in and began setting up the union machinery and passing out literature that the men really learned what the union was all about.

Nowadays, Sid says, "I tell the boys down here at our local that they'd better hold up what they have, because it took a sacrifice of an awful lot of money, time, and blood for us to get the union in this field."

ELIJAH MAYS

Holden, West Virginia.

Fig. 4. Elijah Mays, Holden, WV, 1974 (*United Mine Workers Journal*, January 16–31, 1974. Used by permission.)

E lijah Mays was born in 1902 on a farm in rural Ellis County, Kentucky. At fifteen, he quit school and left home to look for work. "There wasn't any reason to stay in school," he says, "and we were poor people, and in those days, we needed all the money coming in we could just to keep the family fed." He came first to the Big Coal River in central West Virginia where he found work on a saw logging job. Two years later, like so many young men then, he came to the booming Logan coalfields and found a job setting timber at the Island Creek mines at Omar. He worked as a miner in Logan County until his retirement in 1965, "doing," as he puts it, "everything in the mines there was to do."

Elijah says that he has been a union man for about so long as he can remember. In 1921, a deputy sheriff came down to Omar to recruit miners there to fight against the union on Blair Mountain.

But Elijah knew right away that he wouldn't take up arms against a union brother. "He just come down there," he recalls, "and told us to get on down to the courthouse and pick us up some high-powered rifles and go up on the mountains to fight. But there was a bunch of us there, five or six of us, that was boarding there together, and we were all from around the same place in Kentucky, you know, and we was all union men at heart. Well, we wouldn't go, not a one of us. This deputy told us we couldn't board any train in Logan County, but we said, 'You just try and stop us!' It was just like the wild west, you know, and we took our pistols and loaded our families onto the train there and went over to Kentucky until it was all over.

"I'd say that about ninety-five percent of the miners here in Logan County was union men at heart, even ten years before the union come in here, but they didn't have the right to organize, and they didn't have no leader. If anyone in the mines started talking about the union or if an organizer came in here, well, these deputies would just take him off to jail. Don Chafin, he was the sheriff in here at that time, he kept deputies in here for that very purpose. They say, but I don't know it for a fact, that the coal operators paid him ten cents on the ton to pay them. Now, that's just hearsay, you know. Some of these organizers he had shot. And some of them, I've heard, he even had burned up in that powerhouse over in Logan.

"Around the end of the twenties was when the union spirit really began to take a hold among the miners. Things were real hard in here at that time. Men was having a hard time feeding their families. They was only working one, two, maybe three days a week. They cleaned up a lot of the hillsides around here and raised gardens so that they could feed themselves. And they were cutting wages too. In 1931, I finally had to quit my job and go back to Kentucky for a few months, because I wasn't even making enough to pay my board. I was paying twenty dollars a month board, and I was only drawing about seven fifty for a two-week pay period. I was working on the drilling machine at the time, and when they cut our pay from six cents a car to four cents, well, I then knew that I just couldn't make it and that I'd have to leave.

"Well, it was just about a year later, I think, that the UMW sent the first organizers in here to Logan to talk with the men. There was two of them sent down here, Lee Hall, and I don't know the other one's name. Well, they come over to Whitman Creek, where I was at that time, and there was a deputy waiting for them, and he was aiming to arrest them just as soon as they set one foot on company property. But those organizers knew better than to do that. Well, the men had been waiting for it, and it wasn't just a little while before they'd all signed up. They'd been waiting for it for a long time.

"Well, after that, things just began going better, and we was getting three dollars for a car of coal that we'd have gotten eighty-five cents on a couple of years before."

FRANK DEEN

Holden, West Virginia

F rank Deen immigrated from Italy to the United States in 1920. He lived for two years in Baltimore, his point of entry, and then came to Logan County to find work in the mines. He married a locally born coal miner's daughter, settled in Holden, and spent the rest of his working life as an employee of the Island Creek Coal Company. Today, he lives in his own home, a former "company house," which he bought from Island Creek with his savings. Frank considers himself fully an American, although he still speaks with a heavy, sensuously rich, Mediterranean accent.

Frank clearly remembers the early years of the Depression. "We had plenty of hardship," he says. "We was living in shacks, almost cardboard shacks, you might say. And we weren't hardly making enough to eat, and everyone was tending a little vegetable garden, growing tomatoes, and beans, and corn, and all, you know. And, they'd can it to last them through the winter. You should have seen these hillsides around here, it was just one little patch after another.

"Right about '28, they started cutting wages. I remember that real good. I had a superintendent, Charlie Adkins, and he called me 'Buddy.' He called everyone 'Buddy.' One day, he says to me,

'Buddy, how much do you think you're making for that car of coal?'
I says, 'Ninety cents.' I knew I was making ninety cents for it, that
was our wages. 'No,' he says, 'you're getting eighty-five cents for
that car of coal.' He was telling me my wages was being cut! They
kept cutting. That was just the beginning. Then it went to eighty
cents, then seventy-five. We wasn't making more than five fifty
a day on our best days, and we wasn't working but a couple days
a week then."

But it wasn't as if there were any alternatives open to Frank.
"When Charlie said that to me," Frank continues, his voice rising
for dramatic effect, "I said, 'You can't do that to me! I earned
ninety-five cents on that car of coal. I'm leaving, I'm quitting,
that's all!' But you know what Charlie says to me then? He says,
'Well, Buddy, you can go if you want, but you're not going to find
nothing better.' Well, I saw that he was right. Of course, I could
have maybe become a mine foreman or a superintendent and
made more money that way. But to do that, you needed a high
school diploma at least, and I didn't have one, and if there was
any way that you could get one without quitting your job and
starving, nobody ever told me about it. Well, I'm telling you, I
just felt about like a slave.

"Well, when Mr. Roosevelt commenced being president, he
gave us the right to organize, and he said he was behind every
working man's getting what was his due. That's when the organizers started coming down here and speaking with us. They was just
all coal miners, like us, really, you know. This one fellow, Justice
was his name, was a coal miner from over on Coal River. Well, we
heard on the radio that there was going to be a meeting, and we
all went over to the ballpark. Well, I'm telling you, I liked it. We
had been hoping this would happen, and we agreed with these
speakers one hundred percent."

"Now, we did have one problem. The company knew these
laws before we did, and they tried to start up one of these company unions. Well, we didn't know the difference and a lot of the

men signed up. But there was this one fellow that I worked with that saw through it. 'Why now?' he says. 'Why does the company want us to join the union now when they've been fighting us all these years? What kind of union can this be? The United Mine Workers—that's the union we need!' Well, we knew that he was right, and we was behind the UMW all the way after that."

SPENCER MULLINS AND LAURA ADKINS MULLINS

Verdunville, West Virginia

S pencer Mullins went to work for the Rossmore Coal Company at Omar in the early twenties loading coal. He has worked in the mines virtually ever since, being "a general handy-man, you know, I could load, or lay track, or run a motor rig, or shoot, or just about anything that needed doing."

Today, Spencer and his wife Laura live in their own home on Mud Fork. The home is filled with pictures of their two sons, whom they were able to put through school, and who are now working as mine inspectors.

No one had even heard of a union in Logan County before World War I. But after Spencer returned from duty in France and entered the mines, he began to hear some talk, mostly from miners who had come down to Logan from the northern fields to find work. But generally, he remembers, people kept pretty quiet about it, because if one of Chafin's deputies overheard any union talk, that would be the end of the man's job.

It was during the years of the Depression that union sentiment really began to build up. This is how Spencer describes it: "It took us a good two years to get this field organized. The further along it got, the more people were for it. People would go around door to door, talking about the union, and they'd say, 'Well, how about meeting over at so-and-so's house.' And then maybe they'd get five, six, eight, ten, twelve, fifteen men to agree, and first thing you'd know, they'd all feel a little braver and would get so that they'd feel like they would dare meet. Of course, we couldn't let anybody know about these meetings. They was real secret.

"Our bunch, we used to meet down the road here about two miles, at Bill Tiller's place. We picked that because he owned his own house, and we weren't going to have no coal company thugs prowling around. Well, that little house was where I first took that union obligation, and I remember that well.

"The way I see it, the more we got into it, the braver we felt. And, after a few years, it had gotten along enough so that they could take care of themselves.

"And then, when the district officers commenced coming down here and calling meetings, well, then it come along real good."

Laura talked for a while about life in the mining camps where she lived for most of her life and where she raised her children. Although there were some things about the camps—the crowding, the fact that the company owned all the houses—that she disliked, she remembers other things about the camps with great pleasure. "Everyone just got along like one big happy family," she remembered.

Today, the Mullins, with his union pension, are living fairly well. "But I wish," Laura says, "that we'd had this money back in the early thirties, when I was raising our children. That's when we really needed it. Now, we're sick, and can't get out much. What we have now we could have used then. But, that's all through with, I guess."

SHIRLEY WORKMAN

Mud Fork, West Virginia

S hirley Workman's husband, Isaac, now eighty-five years old, worked in Island Creek Coal Company mines in Logan County for close to forty years.

Isaac joined the union, Shirley remembers, "over fifty-four years ago, I'd say, well, it was before that trouble on Blair Mountain." But the men had a hard time getting the operators to recognize their organization. "The sheriffs, and all of them, were against it, you know," she says. "And they were the law. Back in those days, you know, no God-fearing person would go against the law. The miners were just afraid, as near as I can figure it."

Instead of challenging outright the powerful coal operators and their deputies, men like Isaac Workman kept their union sympathies to themselves. Even Shirley wasn't exactly sure when her husband joined the union, "because that was something that he didn't tell nobody."

According to his wife, Isaac had felt a strong sense of loyalty to the union. "They had a kind of vow to each other, I guess you might say, that they'd stick together in time of troubles. If they backed down, I guess they just weren't good union men."

To Shirley, the coal industry has been an impersonal force, one that has valued production over human values. She ought to know. Her husband and two of her ten children have been disabled by lung illnesses caused by work in the mines. Another son died, at age thirty-two, in the explosion at the Island Creek mine No. 22 at Holden ten years ago. "Them big bosses," she says, in the measured words of someone who has learned to suffer silently, "don't seem to care very much, so long as they get their coal."

RICHARD BURGETT

Monaville, West Virginia

R ichard Burgett doesn't show his true colors right away. He sits in his rather conventional living room—decorated with religious icons, a TV set, plastic flowers, and several baroque vases—in Monaville, and piously tells his interviewer that he'll be happy to answer any question as best he can. But within half an hour, he is, with a wicked gleam in his eye, rocking back and forth in his armchair chanting old organizing ballads, pulling old carbide lamps out of dusty bureau drawers, and shooting mine guards with imaginary machine guns. Much to the amazement, it must be added, of his wife, who has watched the whole transformation with no small measure of bewilderment.

In 1920, the United Mine Workers succeeded in organizing Mingo County for the first time, and the miners went out on strike for union recognition. Richard had already known about the union for some time. In 1917, he had met the locally born organizer, Morgan Justice, in the mines. "I guess that the union got in touch with him to help them organize because they knew he wasn't afraid of nothing and would tell the company just what he thought of them," he reflected. Richard was already in sympathy with the union position. "I was working at the time on the cutting machine," he recalls.

"Well, I took the obligation on Saturday, and we was thrown out on Monday. They told us we'd have to get out or sign the yaller-dog, one or t'other."[1] Whole camps were evicted, and tent colonies sprang up in Chattaroy, Lick Creek, and Goodman. The union, the men, and the operators, all were determined to fight to the end what they, correctly, saw to be a test case of the relative strength of the union and management in the southern West Virginia coalfields.

The strike lasted two years, was bitterly contested, and ended finally in the rout of the union. Coal operators brought in strike-breakers "on transportation." ("You didn't need no skill in those days," Richard says. "Just about anybody could shovel or take a breast auger and drill and shoot down the coal.") Scabs who made it past the sign at the railroad depot ("Be advised that there is a strike in progress. Those who choose to return to Huntington will have their way paid by the company.") sometimes didn't make it to the mines, because they were waylaid by angry strikers.

The company employed private detective agencies and mine guards to terrorize the men and the union workers. A group of armed guards ambushed and fired upon a small group of union organizers making their way through the woods. The attackers allegedly seized the already badly mutilated body of one of their victims, the organizer Alex Breedlove,[2] tied it to the back of an automobile, and dragged the corpse along dirt roads all the way to Williamson. The miners were incensed. Nearly the entire working community turned out for the funeral. The line of mourners

---

1 A "yellow-dog" contract refers to an agreement between an employer and a worker that the worker will not join or retain membership in a union. Some employers made hiring or continued employment contingent on the worker signing such a contract.
2 Alex Breedlove was an African American union miner born in Pike County, Kentucky, in 1889. A well-known figure in the community, his killing at the hands of West Virginia State Police during their raid of the Lick Creek Tent Colony on June 14, 1921, set off a wave of grief and rage among the miners of southern West Virginia, which contributed to their eventual March on Blair Mountain in August of that year.

following the casket to the cemetery, Richard estimates, stretched three quarters of a mile long.

In a time of such raw class warfare, it was not easy for the public officials to maintain a position of neutrality. Sheriff Blankenship of Mingo County had tried; he had refused to allow the coal companies to determine the selection of deputies, as in Logan County. "I ain't going to appoint no criminals or murderers to be public officials in *this* county," he was reputed to have said. His successor, A. C. Pinson, however, did things differently. Although he had run on a platform of continuing the policies of his predecessor, during his first week in office, the coal company offered him fifteen thousand dollars to allow them to mount machine guns in a store front overlooking Matewan's Main Street. Pinson said yes, Richard reported. "It's not too surprising," he added, "considering what they offered him."

While the men were out on strike, the organizers, Richard remembers, used to sing songs to keep up the morale. Although he at first declined to remember ("Aw, you shouldn't have reminded me of that!"), Richard finally sang one of these songs, at first tentatively, and then again for a second and third time, with great enthusiasm and pleasure. The lyrics went something like this:

> Where's old Armentraut when the hailstorm comes, just as
>   easy,
> Grabbed him a rifle and away he's run.
> Marvin Lambert's done the same,
> With his hair hanging down like a yaller-dogs's mane.
> Jim Bowalters, called him a mighty brave man,
> He's got a brave body, but his legs won't stand.

Armentraut, Lambert, and Bowalters, Richard explains, were local coal operators. "Old Tom Parsons wrote the song," he points out, "to show up what cowards these men was at heart." Morgan Justice had another favorite, the well-known industrial ballad, "The

Hard-Working Miner," in which he'd substitute local incidents for the more general lyrics of the original. In his version, the miner was "Old George, who died on the tipple."

The Mingo County miners might have won their strike if the Battle of Blair Mountain had been successful. It wasn't. Richard didn't fight in it—there was no way for the Mingo County miners to join their union brothers on Blair Mountain without passing through the company-dominated Logan County—but the striking miners were very aware of what went on there. Richard had heard of the shooting of John Gore, and the capture of the Mitchell brothers and Howard Young by the miners, and of the exploits of Bad Lewis White. He knew, too, why the march had failed. It was, quite plainly, "because they sent the army in there to break it up."

In 1926, Richard moved to Logan County and entered the mines there. Towards the end of the decade, wages started declining, and Richard found it hard to support his family. By 1932, he was making around thirty-five dollars a month, paid in scrip, most of which went to pay off old debts to the company. He, like others, began to roam the countryside looking for work. "It was just beans and bread one day, and bread and beans the next," he says of these years.

Finally, in 1933, the union began, with the support of sympathetic federal legislation, to make headway in the southern coalfields. Morgan Justice, who by some miracle was still alive, was back again for his second try. "All the demons in Hell," he told his friend Richard, "can't keep us from organizing Logan County now." As Richard remembers, the owners of the No. 22 Holden mine, where he was working at the time, tried to co-opt union sentiment by forming a company union and appointing the most active miners to prestigious positions on the mine committees. The ploy aborted. Richard was so anxious to join the UMWA that he took off in the middle of the night to take the obligation. "I was," he chuckles, "going to sign up before anyone could make me get into any old company union!" It wasn't long before all the other miners there followed suit.

Richard couldn't resist singing one more ballad before his interviewer left.

Once in my saddle, I used to go dashing,
Once in my saddle, I used to ride gay.
First, I got drinking, then I got gambling,
I got shot in the bosom, and I'm dying today.

He laughed roundly.

ALBERT WILLIAMSON

Verdunville, West Virginia

A lbert Williamson, now sixty-eight years old, began working in the mines in Logan County when he was sixteen, and has worked in virtually every mine in the county. He retired in 1956, when his back was broken in a slate fall. "If it hadn't been for my getting all butchered up like that," he says, "I'd still be mining today."

Back during the Depression, Albert recalls, "men weren't making more than only seventy cents on a car of coal. And many a time, we'd have to do hours of work cleaning up the dirt and slate and not get paid anything for it. But you couldn't complain. We had our bosses in the mines—cut-bosses, they called them then—and they'd tell you, if you didn't do just what they said, well, there was plenty of men waiting on the outside for your job. So, these miners had to work day and night to hold on to their jobs.

"Of course, we all wanted the union, but we couldn't get it, we had to wait. When it first come in here, when Roosevelt give us the right to organize, the companies was against it. We had to have our meeting outside of their property, you know. But once it got going, the companies was behind it just like everybody else. The company goes along with it now, and I think they even like it.

"I tell a lot of the young people now about that we went through. I think if the young people knew about it, they'd try harder to hold it up. I wish everybody like you would try and get out and learn about these things."

NATHAN ENGLAND

Monaville, West Virginia

B orn in 1905 in Tennessee, Nathan England entered the non-union Ravenscroft mines near his home at the age of sixteen.
Times were hard in the mines before the union was organized. Back when he first started working, Nathan recalls, "if you didn't do exactly what the boss said for you to do regardless of what it was, you were just out and gone. You didn't have no backing." Men were plentiful and jobs were scarce. The men were afraid to back their buddies for fear they would lose their own jobs. The men were paid $1.25 for what often amounted to an eighteen-hour shift. Many weeks, the men would not see their children until Sunday. "We had this kind of fear, all the time," he recalls, "about whether we would make it to the next day or not."

By 1923, pro-union sentiment in the mine was beginning to "kindle up." But the company would not stand behind it, and the men were too poor to sustain a prolonged strike. So, they began having secret union meetings. "We'd go way out, where the company had no authority, away from the town, just like we was going hunting or something. We didn't have any shoot-out battles like they did in this part of the country," he concludes, "but it sure was a whole lot of trouble."

The men did not win their rights to collective bargaining for another ten years. In 1933, Roosevelt signed the National Industrial Recovery Act, and the operators finally were forced to recognize the union. The men held a huge rally in the local ballpark. The union officers came down from Knoxville. They roasted beans and hogs and generally, Nathan says, "had a big time." He added, "If you're down and out, and you see something that'll be of some benefit to you, it'll cheer you up. It just seemed like it put a smile on the miner's face to see something that could benefit not just him, but everybody that was working in the coal mines. One of the happiest days I've ever had in my life"—and here Nathan smiles broadly—"was the day I finally signed that union card.

"It took a little while for everyone to understand exactly what the union would mean to the working class of people," he maintains. But, once it did, it benefited the operators as much as it did the men. Things kind of quieted down in the mines after they were organized. Grievances were settled by the mine committees, and the men rarely went out on strike. Things generally, Nathan says, "went pretty smooth, like."

Nathan later worked for the Island Creek Coal Company at Mallory, Monniker, and Holden until 1969, when he was injured in a mine accident and was forced to retire.

Nathan asked quite a few questions himself during the interview and was very excited about the possibilities of oral history. "I hope that the work you're doing," he told his interviewer, "not just what I've said, but what all of them have said, will influence the young person today. These younger miners, that make fifty dollars a day, they don't know what us old timers went through to get this union. More young people ought to get out and talk to old folks and get their ideas. You can't imagine what kind of good this will do."

AFTERWORD

When I read this book, I was blown away by Anne's ability to connect to these coal mining families who were told that to even speak of a union meant losing their jobs, losing their homes, losing their livelihoods, and sometimes losing their very lives. The notion that I can today be the head of the UMWA is a testament to their determination to organize the union in the face of tremendous repression.

I was born way up the holler of Cabin Creek. My uncle, Bill Blizzard, fought in the battles of Paint Creek and Cabin Creek. He led the UMWA forces at the Battle of Blair Mountain. My great-grandmother, Sarah Blizzard, fought alongside Mother Jones. I have heard stories my entire life about the days before the union, which is why I have dedicated everything within me to UMWA members and their families. Which is why Anne's manuscript is so important to me. Being able to document what these families went through and how these miners felt can help preserve a history that I am afraid, if we're not vigilant, may very well repeat itself if we let it.

In any all-out struggle, you are going to win and you are going to lose, but without these conflicts, without these miners rising up, the United Mine Workers of America would never have become, by 1935, the largest union in the United States. We owe a lot to those miners who were willing to march on Blair Mountain, those miners who fought the Baldwin-Felts thugs in Paint Creek and Cabin Creek and who refused to back down in Matewan. People died so that others could have this union, and without those efforts, without all of the sacrifices that have taken place since the formation of the United Mine Workers in 1890, I truly do not believe we would have the middle class we have today.

It is so important to keep our history alive and that is what this book does. It documents the struggles those who formed the union had to go through. It brings to life the fear that was part of these miners' everyday existence, simply because they wanted to be treated like free human beings with respect and fairness on the job.

Luther Keen, whose story appears in this book, put it perfectly, "You may have been for the union, but brother, you'd better not mention it, because they were tough on anyone was known to be leaning towards the union. They didn't care nothing for a man's life." No miner has been given anything; we have had to fight for every single thing we have. That was true 100 years ago and it still stands true today.

Cecil E. Roberts
UMWA International President

SELECTED EDUCATIONAL RESOURCES

FILMS

Blood on the Mountain, 2016
Even the Heavens Weep, 1985
Matewan, 1987
The Mine Wars, 2016

BOOKS

Bailey, Rebecca J. *Matewan before the Massacre: Politics, Coal, and the Roots of Conflict in a West Virginia Mining Community*. Morgantown: West Virginia University Press, 2008.

Corbin, David Alan. *Gun Thugs, Rednecks, and Radicals: A Documentary History of the West Virginia Mine Wars*. Oakland: PM Press, 2011.

Corbin, David Alan. *Life, Work, and Rebellion in the Coalfields: The Southern West Virginia Miners, 1880–1922*. 2nd ed. Morgantown: West Virginia University Press, 2015.

Eller, Ronald. *Miners, Millhands, and Mountaineers: Industrialization of the Appalachian South, 1880–1930*. Knoxville: University of Tennessee, 1982.

Fones-Wolf, Ken and Ronald L. Lewis, eds., *Transnational West Virginia: Ethnic Communities and Economic Change, 1840–1940*. Morgantown: West Virginia University Press, 2002.

Giardina, Denise. *Storming Heaven: A Novel.* Toronto: Ivy Books, 1988.

Green, James. *The Devil Is Here in These Hills: West Virginia's Coal Miners and Their Battle for Freedom.* New York: Atlantic Monthly Press, 2015.

Hess, J. W., ed. *Struggle in the Coal Fields: The Autobiography of Fred Mooney.* Morgantown: West Virginia University Library, 1967.

Lewis, Ronald L. *Black Coal Miners in America: Race, Class, and Community Conflict.* Lexington: University Press of Kentucky, 2015.

Lunt, Richard D. *Law and Order vs. the Miners: West Virginia, 1907–1933.* Hamden, CT: Archon Books, 1979.

Savage, Lon. *Thunder in the Mountains: The West Virginia Mine War, 1920–21.* Pittsburgh: University of Pittsburgh Press, 1990.

Shogan, Robert. *The Battle of Blair Mountain: The Story of America's Largest Labor Uprising.* New York: Basic Books, 2006.

Sullivan, Ken, ed. *The Goldenseal Book of the West Virginia Mine Wars.* 1991. Reprint, Charleston, WV: Quarrier Books, 2020.

Trotter, Joe William. *Coal, Class, and Color: Blacks in Southern West Virginia, 1915–32.* Urbana: University of Illinois Press, 1990.

Wilkerson, Jessica. *To Live Here, You Have to Fight: How Women Led Appalachian Movements for Social Justice.* Urbana: University of Illinois Press, 2019.

ON THE WEB

"Beneath the Surface and Cast in Steel: Forging the American Industrial Union Movement," Penn State University Libraries: https://sites.psu.edu/industrialunionism/

"Blair Pathways: A Musical Exploration of America's Largest Labor Uprising": https://www.blairpathways.com

"Coal Mines, Miners, & Labor," PBS Learning Media: https://www.pbslearningmedia.org/collection/west-virginia-coal-mines-and-miners

"Labor," West Virginia Archives & History: http://www.wvculture.org/history/labor/labor.html

"Teacher Resources," The West Virginia Mine Wars Museum: https://www.wvminewars.com/teacher-resources

GOVERNMENT DOCUMENTS

Conditions in the Paint Creek District, West Virginia: Hearings before a Subcommittee of the Committee on Education and Labor, U.S. Senate, 63rd Congress, first session, pursuant to S. res. 37, 1913 (full text: https://catalog.hathitrust.org/Record/008606894)

West Virginia Coal Fields: Hearings before the Committee on Education and Labor, U.S. Senate, 67th. Congress, first session, pursuant to S. Res. 80, 1921 (full text: https://catalog.hathitrust.org/Record/008610716)

ARCHIVAL COLLECTIONS

William Blizzard Collection, West Virginia State Archives, Ms 97–24, Charleston, WV

H. C. Lewis Collection (Papers of Baldwin-Felts Detective Agency founder Thomas L. Felts), Eastern Regional Coal Archives, 90–129, Craft Memorial Library, Bluefield, WV

Miners' Treason Trials Records, West Virginia & Regional History Center, A&M 0979, West Virginia University, Morgantown, WV

United Mine Workers of America Records, Eberly Family Special Collections Library, Penn State University, State College, PA

ORAL HISTORIES

Anne T. Lawrence Mine Workers Oral History Collection, George Washington University Special Collections Research Center, Washington, D.C.

Matewan Oral History Project Collection, West Virginia Archives & History, Charleston, WV

Transcripts of Interviews, *Even the Heavens Weep*, West Virginia Archives & History, Charleston, WV, and online at http://www.wvculture.org/history /labor/evenheavensweep.html

West Virginia & Regional History Center Oral History Collection, West Virginia University, Morgantown, WV

INDEX

Depression, life during, 108
as deputy sheriff, 108
Don Chafin, friendship with, 108
early organizing, remembering,
111
Lillybrook mine, working in, 109
logging, 108
machines, working with, 110
miners, on equality of, 111
Mud Fork, 107
Raycore mines, working in, 109
"trouble on Blair Mountain,"
107–8
Dun Glen Hotel, 16

Elkhorn, Kentucky, 66
England, Nathan
Island Creek Coal Company,
working for, 148
operators rally, 148
pro-union sentiment, 147
Ravenscroft mines, working in,
147
Epps, Willie
Depression, life before, 104
Ernie, 16–17, 22
See also Jackson, Grace
Eskdale, 15

First World War, 26, 66, 80

Gay Coal and Coke Company, 100
Gazette, 72
Ghiz, John
Logan, first confectioner of, 75
work, looking for, 74
Ghiz, Mary, 74–75
Gore, Elbert
on Battle of Blair Mountain,
58–59
Blair Mountain, patrolling, 55
on Captain Brockus, 58–59
on coal companies, 57

on coal mines, 57
father, death of, 61
and Hewett Creek, 60
on Hossie, 62
on Kanawha County, 57–58
on Lewis White, 60
as schoolteacher, 56
sheriffdom, tradition of, 56
and Sunday school, 56
suspicions of, 56, 60
Gore, John, 38, 41, 55, 67, 81,
143
Gothard, William "Bill," 87
on Don Chafin, 84–85
as neutral, 83–84
on Old Boss Payne, 84
on self, 86
trapper, working as, 83
as union man, 84
Great Depression, 7, 54, 104,
108–9, 113, 124, 133, 136,
145
Green, James, 2
Guyandotte River, 4, 6, 8, 95

Hager, Ira
brother, death of, 105
cases, handling of, 105
on "Cleveland Panic," 104
coal industry, breaking, 105–6
education, 104
"keeping the books," 104–5
learning to read, 104–5
work, praise of, 106
Harding, Warren G., 1, 6
"Hard-Working Miner, The" (song),
143
Harlow, Lana Blizzard
boarding house, 46
"breeding mark," 47
on father, 45–46
on gender roles, 46
on miners, 46–47
on siblings, 46
strikes, remembering, 46

Hatfield, Devil Anse, 87
Hatfield, Henry D., 17
Hatfield, Sid, 5, 27, 35, 40, 88, 117
Hatfield, Tennis, 9
Hatfield, Will, 88
Herald Dispatch, 72
Holden No. 7 mine, 113
Hossie, 62
Huntington Herald, 27
Hurt, Bill, 38

Island Creek Coal Company, 34, 66–67, 92, 115, 128, 133, 138, 148

Jackson, Grace, 15
  on "Bill Hickok days," 16
  Cabin Creek, remembering, 17–18
  Cabin Creek Strike, women during, 21
  on Dirty Aunt Nellie, 17
  and fishing, 16
  on Mother Jones, 18
  quilts, crafting, 15–16
  rights, fighting for, 15
Johnson, Lee
  Don Chafin, remembering, 123
  early life of, 123
  trade unionism, understanding, 124
  and union obligation, 124
  union sympathy, 124–25
Johnson, Tom, 93
Jones, Mary "Mother." *See* Mother Jones
Jones, Pinhead
  early life of, 91–92
  Franklin Roosevelt, 92
  John L. Lewis, 92
Josephs, T. R., 31
Justice, Morgan, 140, 142–43
Justice of the Peace (J.P.), 63

Kanawha City, West Virginia, 96
Kanawha County, 3, 4, 15, 49, 54, 57
  coalfield, 1, 5, 7, 43, 72
  Kanawha River, 38, 64
  Kanawha Valley, 43
Keen, Luther
  on Don Chafin, 113
  Island Creek, working at, 112
  miners' march, recalling, 112–13
  organizing drive, assisting in, 113–14
  union forces, remembering, 112
Keeney, Frank, 44
Kemp, Eli, 41
Kinser, Otis, 121–22
Knights of Labor, 45

Lambert, Marvin, 142
Lewis, John L., 47, 90, 92, 106, 128
Lick Creek Tent Colony, 141
Literal, Charles
  on Baldwin-Felts agents, 88–89
  on Battle of Blair Mountain, 90
  on Billy Foster, 87
  Devil Anse Hatfield, visiting grave of, 87
  and Jimmy Damron, 88
  on Mother Jones, 90
  on Sid Hatfield, 88
  on Sid's wife, 89
Lively, Charlie E., 29
Logan Banner, 72
Logan County
  Battle of Blair Mountain, surrounding communities during, 7–8
  miners, 21, 68
  newspapers, 55, 94
  union in, 106, 135
  unionization, patterns of, 3
  union organizers sweeping through, 9
Logan Senior Citizens Hospitality Center, 91

Wilburn, James, 81
Wilburn, John
  Battle of Blair Mountain,
    time during, 41
  on Bill Blizzard, 40–41
  on Holly Smith, 39
  on Mingo County strike,
    40
  Omar, working at, 38
  on Sid Hatfield, 40
  union, organizing, 39
  "wildcat," setting off, 94
wildcat strike, 119
Williamson, Albert
  Depression, recalling, 145
  Logan County mines,
    working in, 145
  union, wanting, 145–46

Williamson County, 2–4, 27, 58,
  97, 119–20, 141
Wise County, Virginia, 120
Workman, Isaac
  loyalty, 138–39
  union, joining, 138
Workman, Shirley, 138–39
Wyoming County, 3–4

"yellow-dog," 18, 141
Young, Howard, 63–64
Young, Octavia
  on Battle of Blair Mountain,
    63–64
  on Howard Young, 63–64
  Logan, arriving in, 63
  on mine work, 63–64

Printed in the USA
CPSIA information can be obtained
at www.ICGtesting.com
LVHW022252181223
766853LV00047B/1439